Advance Praise for *Counsel, the Courtroom Is Open*

"Zauderer is one of the country's great lawyers and a trusted advisor. His book is a must read for anyone who touches complex litigation, whether in trials or appeals."

—Richard Grasso, former Chairman,
New York Stock Exchange

"*Counsel, the Courtroom Is Open* describes the compelling personal and professional journey of a singularly talented lawyer that serves as a testament to the enduring virtues of the legal profession. This fascinating read provides lessons and insights for attorneys new and old into the world of the practicing lawyer and the joy and personal fulfillment that a career in the law can bring."

—Hon. Jonathan Lippman, Chief Judge
of the State of New York, retired

"This highly readable volume chronicles the remarkable life and career of one of New York's most respected lawyers. Zauderer's fifty years at the forefront of complex commercial litigation and dispute resolution—guided by his exceptional skill and commitment to ethical advocacy— have left an indelible mark on the legal profession. *Counsel, the Courtroom Is Open* is a rich and inspiring read—an enduring tribute to a career built on service, mentorship and the highest ideals of our profession."

—Hon. Janet DiFiore, Chief Judge of
the State of New York, retired

"We are grateful for Zauderer's service and the contribution this book makes to our practice and understanding of the law. As an arbitrator and experienced trial lawyer, he shares insights on how to resolve disputes and how to relate to jurors. An easy and gratifying read."

—Hon. Sol Wachtler, Chief Judge of
the State of New York, retired

"An inspiring and entertaining saga of a great career in the law. It belongs on the bookshelf with the memoirs of Darrow, Nizer, and other outstanding litigators."

—Hon. Howard Levine, Associate Judge,
New York Court of Appeals, retired

"The author has worked with titans of business, our most brilliant legal scholars, and notable members of our revered judiciary. What he shares with the reader is pure wisdom. You need not be a lawyer to learn from this engaging, insightful memoir."

—Hon. Karen Peters, Presiding Justice,
New York Supreme Court, Appellate
Division, Third Department, retired

"A fascinating chronicle of the author's life as he navigated the halls of power while shaping our noble profession for over half a century. His story exemplifies the kind of grace and leadership that should inspire the next generation of lawyers."

—Hon. Rolando Acosta, Presiding Justice,
New York Supreme Court, Appellate
Division, First Department, retired

"Preeminent trial lawyer Mark Zauderer opens the door on his extraordinary career, sharing his personal story and the behind-the-scenes perspective of his groundbreaking cases. In language that is both warm and engaging, Mark shares the lessons of his lifetime, lessons which should be taken to heart by lawyers and their clients alike. Mark traces his journey from childhood in Brooklyn to the courtrooms and boardrooms of high-stakes corporate litigation, leaving the reader enthralled, entertained, and inspired by his achievements and his message."

—Hon. Alan Scheinkman, Presiding Justice,
New York Supreme Court, Appellate
Division, Second Department, retired

"Mark's knowledge of, and experiences in, the New York court system—particularly in complex commercial matters—are unmatched. His book gives readers a behind-the-scenes look at a fifty-year legal practice that includes his work on some of the highest-profile litigations in the country. It is an easy, enjoyable, and educational read."

—Joseph Petrosinelli, Chairman, Williams & Connolly LLP, Washington, DC

"Required reading for anyone seeking a distinguished lawyer's firsthand account of how courtroom battles impact American history and our understanding of the rule of law."

—Kenneth R. Feinberg, Administrator of the 9/11 Victim Compensation Fund of 2001, Washington, DC

"This beautifully written book will show any reader what a joy it is to practice law and to provide the highest form of public service to the bench and bar. In countless matters, the most respected judges and the most demanding clients asked for Mark Zauderer's assistance. He is a true hero of the New York bar, and this book is required reading for anyone aspiring to a career as a litigator, not only in New York but in any court in the nation."

—Kathleen M. Sullivan, former dean of Stanford Law School and partner, Quinn Emanuel Urquhart & Sullivan, LLP, retired

COUNSEL, THE COURTROOM IS OPEN

Lessons from More Than a Half Century in Law and Life

MARK C. ZAUDERER

Post Hill Press

A POST HILL PRESS BOOK
ISBN: 979-8-89565-488-0
ISBN (eBook): 979-8-89565-489-7

Counsel, the Courtroom Is Open:
Lessons from More Than a Half-Century in Law and Life

Cover design by Jim Villaflores

This is a work of nonfiction. All people, locations, events, and situations are portrayed to the best of the author's memory.

Post Hill Press
New York • Nashville
posthillpress.com

Published in the United States of America
1 2 3 4 5 6 7 8 9 10

For Daniel

The author's profits from this book will go entirely to Grassroots Grocery, a 501(c)(3) organization helping people in need. Grassrootsgrocery.org

If a man does not keep pace with his companions, perhaps it is because he hears a different drummer. Let him step to the music which he hears, however measured or far away.

Henry David Thoreau

TABLE OF CONTENTS

PREFACE

In the title of this book are the words that greet lawyers in dozens of courtrooms every morning in New York City, as court officers unlock the doors so that litigants can seek justice. For over fifty years, I have walked through these doors to enter this world. Unfortunately, we live in a world filled with conflict. It is part of the human condition. Whether in the arena of international politics, business, family relationships, or financial transactions, strife and disagreement are givens—and lawyers are usually at the front line. In this book, I want to share with you my experiences in that world.

Until recently, penning an autobiography was one of the last projects I would have thought to undertake. Some twenty years ago, I was privileged to have extended conversations with the former Governor of New York, Mario Cuomo. At the time, I was President of a leading bar association known as the Federal Bar Council. Cuomo was preparing a speech he planned to give at the major annual event of that organization—one that every year would fill the Grand Ballroom of New York's Waldorf-Astoria Hotel, where almost two thousand lawyers and federal judges would celebrate Thanksgiving. It had been many years since

Cuomo had made a major speech to so many lawyers. Cuomo went back and forth with me as he drafted his speech. Was it too long? Too controversial? Too serious?

When Cuomo was satisfied that he had struck the right tone, he spent almost an hour inquiring about my own life. Then, he said, "Mark, you should write your autobiography." Although I was flattered at the suggestion, I never took it seriously. It was only when my son Daniel revived this forgotten idea twenty years later ("Dad, why don't you write your autobiography?") that I started to put pen to paper.

Over the past half century, I have tried cases and argued appeals not only in New York but throughout the country. I have also served as an arbitrator or mediator in dozens of disputes, both public and private. The reader may be familiar with some of the high-profile trials and appeals in which I have been involved. In other instances, I could not reveal details of these cases while they were pending.

In the pages that follow, I will share with you the story of my professional journey. But in Part One of this book, I have tried to give the reader insight into who I am and what circumstances brought me to the starting point of that journey. This is my story.

ACKNOWLEDGMENTS

I am grateful for the time and effort spent by my colleagues on reading drafts of this book as it evolved. Their reactions and diligent fact-checking were extremely helpful. In particular, I want to thank my partners at Dorf Nelson & Zauderer LLP: Jon A. Dorf, Jonathan B. Nelson, Ira B. Matetsky, Jason T. Cohen, and Grant A. Shehigian. Also, my assistant, Jeanne Godfrey, provided invaluable assistance in preparing the manuscript. Finally, my thanks go to Kris Fischer, former Editor-in-Chief of the *New York Law Journal*, who shared with me her many insights into the world of publishing.

PART ONE
GETTING THERE

CHAPTER 1

A MAN IN A RAINCOAT

It was an unusual day, because it was the rare occasion when my mother met me after school. As we approached the steps of the brownstone in Brooklyn Heights where we lived, a man in a tan raincoat beckoned to my mother. She walked a few steps away from me, spoke with the man for a minute or two, and then met me at the top of the stoop. I asked her who that was, and she brushed off the question with a wave. Little did I know that this encounter would play a large role in my life to come.

*****

I knew that my mother, Dorothy Hammerman, had been born in New York City in 1913. She was raised in Brooklyn in reasonable comfort (in fact, on the internet, there is an archival photo of her in Prospect Park at age twenty-three). Like her father, her mother was a Russian immigrant, who had built a modest business as a seamstress for the wealthy WASP crowd, with a shop at Madison Avenue and East 52nd Street in Manhattan. The family managed to buy a small building on Kingston Avenue in Brooklyn, where they lived upstairs and rented out the commercial space. With this promise of security, Dorothy planned to attend college out of town. However, the Depression hit hard, the dress business failed, and her dream died. But she enrolled in Hunter College in New York City and ended up graduating with honors.

My father's childhood was much less comfortable. Jerome Zauderer was born in 1912 in Philadelphia, before the family moved to Brooklyn. With his brother and his parents, Jerome moved from one cold-water flat to another, just ahead of the city marshal with eviction notices for nonpayment of rent. I learned little about my father's childhood until after his death in 2000, when I found a paper bag with hundred-year-old letters and documents that helped me piece together his early life. I learned from a perfectly preserved official document that my grandfather, Marx Zauderer (for whom I was named), was naturalized in New York City in 1894. Behind this document was a love letter he sent from Philadelphia in April 1902 to Rose Fox that began, "My dear Rose, I cannot wait to arrive in your fair city [New York City] to see you. Each second becomes a minute, each minute becomes an hour and each hour becomes a day." Next, I found an engraved wedding invitation in that same year that read:

Mr. Jacob Fox
and Mr. & Mrs. Mendel Zauderer
respectfully announce the coming wedding of
Miss Rose Fox
to Mr. Marx Zauderer
to take place Sunday, July the sixth

One thousand, nine hundred and two
Four P.M.
At the residence of Rabbi B. L. Levinthal
716 Pine St., Philadelphia, Pa.

Bride's residence:
923 Callowhille Street
Phila, Pa.

I knew that my father's brother, Seymour, was born the next year.

Raised in abject poverty in Brooklyn, my father attended Franklin K. Lane High School, where he frequently encountered members of the Jewish Mafia, who had succeeded the Irish immigrants and preceded the Italian immigrants a decade later. All had mastered the underworld trades. Apparently, intelligence ran in the family. Jerome's brother, Seymour, born in 1903, managed to wrangle himself a full scholarship to Amherst College and then went on to medical school. In 1928, a high-school teacher took an interest in my father and persuaded him to apply to Columbia University, where he was admitted with a full scholarship. But his path was hardly a bed of roses. At that time, Columbia's President, Nicholas Murray Butler, much in line with leaders of that day, was known as an anti-Semite. In fact, he had complained that too many Jews of Eastern European background were being admitted to the college.

Because he had not a dime to his name, Jerome worked nights as a shipping clerk and commuted from Brooklyn to Columbia in Manhattan. After his first year, the stock market crashed, the Depression hit, and these circumstances almost ended his college career. As my father described it, he glided with success through all of his courses at Columbia except one: chemistry. When grades were publicly posted (a common practice in those days), my father saw that he had received a poor grade, which put his scholarship in jeopardy. He went to see the lab assistant who had graded the students' papers and was told, "Zauderer, the head of the Chemistry Department, Professor Carpenter, graded your paper personally."

So, this sixteen-year-old student from an immigrant family made an appointment with Professor Carpenter. The vaunted chemistry professor took out the exam book and went over each question and answer; the answers were binary, so each was either right or wrong. After seeing that the answers were in fact correct, the professor put down the exam book, turned to my father, and said, "Look, Zauderer, you're a Jew, and I don't like Jews. And I'm not going to do anything about this." Fortunately, Jerome's scholarship survived, and he went on to graduate—but not when he expected. In order to continue as a student, Jerome had taken a loan of several hundred dollars from the university. He was scheduled to graduate in 1932 but was unable to pay back the loan until two years later, whereupon Columbia awarded him his degree in the class of 1934. Several times, my father wryly mentioned to me that when alumni representatives of the class of 1934 reached out to him for an alumni contribution, he had to respond that he did not know anyone in the class of 1934.

These were not the only hurdles that Jerome encountered at Columbia. He often recounted how he had approached a student friend who worked in the library and maintained a card catalog with the names of local employers who wanted to hire students part-time. When Jerome asked to see some of the notices, his friend showed him that many of the employers noted, "No Jews or Irish need apply."

Some seventy years later, I was retained by the General Counsel of Columbia to represent the university in a number of legal matters. I was graciously given a pass to park on the east–west walk that traverses the Columbia campus. As I exited my car, I saw young people of just about every race and ethnicity. Before ascending the steps of Low Library, I paused and, in a moment of sadness, wondered if anybody on the campus had any idea of what the university, and indeed the country at large, was like in the 1920s, when anti-immigrant feelings and notions of racial superiority led Congress to close the doors to Eastern European immigration—and when my father almost lost his scholarship.

CHAPTER 2

WORLD WAR II ON A MILITARY BASE

I don't know how my parents met, but at the tail end of the Depression they moved in together—a rather bold step for young people of that generation. They married in 1940. In the depths of the Depression, Jerome had trained himself as an electrical engineer, not earning his master's degree in engineering until after World War II. After the Pearl Harbor attack, Jerome was recruited to head a secret project at Scott Field, a military base in East St. Louis, Illinois. With Germany's development of rockets, the United States was desperate to develop technology that could be used to counter this new, potentially devastating threat. Jerome headed a group of engineers working to develop the proximity fuse, a fledgling computer device to allow defensive missiles to counter offensive rockets when in their "proximity." So that my mother could accompany him on the military base, Jerome taught her basic radio engineering, so she could, in turn, instruct servicemen at Scott Field. Jerome's participation in the early development of computers started him on a lifelong journey as a pioneer in that field. He founded two start-up companies that developed and sold electronic inventions to the U.S. military, and he was granted a number of patents.

CHAPTER 3
LEFT AND BOARDED

During the late 1920s, the salad days of my grandmother's dress-shop business, Dorothy's father purchased ten acres of land in Rockland County, about twenty miles north of the recently built George Washington Bridge (the Tappan Zee Bridge was decades in the future). A large condominium development now sits on what was then my grandfather's undeveloped land. Dorothy's father built on the property what was not much more than a cabin, later wiring it for electricity. During the summer of 1946, while she was on leave from her job at the New York City Housing Authority (where she was in the first class of female managers), Dorothy stayed with me, her infant son, in the family cabin. Perhaps ahead of her time, she had little interest in raising a child full-time and in the fall decided to return to work full-time in New York City.

This decision resulted in what I have been told caused a trauma in my life that still has its effects seventy-five years later. Diagonally across the road from our cabin was a young couple with a seven-year-old daughter. They were in need of income, and the couple offered to board me in order to allow my parents to return to their apartment in Manhattan. My parents left me, visiting me at first on weekends and then less frequently. The arrangement lasted for some two years until my parents reclaimed me when it was time to start nursery school. I have vivid memories of events during that period (my best friend was a chicken, who followed me around the property). I particularly recall one incident at the end of a weekend parental visit, being physically forced against my will to return to the home where I was boarded. Not surprisingly, when I entered nursery school, my social behavior was less than ideal, as I carried with me anger stemming from my early experience. In fact, over the years of school that followed, while my academic performance was stellar, I never managed to earn a grade above C-minus in the category of "Citizenship."

These two years of isolation from my parents left their scars. Although I have spent many of my happiest times by myself, one remnant of the early experience comes to mind. As a young law-firm associate, I spent a weekend with a group of friends at a house in upstate New York. Sleeping later than the others, I awoke to find the house empty, as everybody had gone for an early-morning walk. Although there was no danger, a moment of anxiety gripped me that lasted until I had finished my first cup of coffee. I am sure that many people have similar residues of trauma that are manifested in fears of heights, enclosed places, and the like.

CHAPTER 4

BROOKLYN HEIGHTS

In the 1950s, Brooklyn Heights was a charming, low-key residential community of mid-nineteenth-century brownstones. Sometimes known as the first suburb of Manhattan, the neighborhood was populated by a good number of New York blue bloods and featured many of their favorite institutions, such as the Brooklyn Heights Casino, an exclusive tennis club where I doubt anyone of my family's background could have set foot. The Heights community boasted that the abolitionist Henry Ward Beecher had delivered his fiery sermons there. Several prominent cultural idols, including Truman Capote and playwright Arthur Miller, made their home in the Heights.

In the spring of 1953, as I was completing the second grade in a left-leaning private school in Manhattan (a school thought of as "Communist" at the time), my parents packed up and moved from Manhattan to a brownstone on Remsen Street in Brooklyn Heights, where I would spend the next twenty years. I took an admissions test (I appeared for a required interview at this Quaker school in a cowboy outfit and two holstered cap guns) and was admitted to the third grade in the Brooklyn Friends School, where I remained a student until graduation from high school ten years later. I recall one of the questions on the entrance test. The school psychologist administering the test asked me to imagine that a boy had lost his wallet in a field and wanted to search for it. I was asked to take a pencil and draw the route he should take to ensure he didn't overlook any place where the wallet might be found. I occasionally think about whether my diagram would stand the test of time.

Brooklyn Friends was a remarkable school at the time—an all-encompassing, welcoming environment (my class never had more than twenty-six students) that stressed humane, Quaker values without requiring religious observance. The school was the most significant influence in my life. The education was classical: For two years in the seventh and eighth grades, the students in English class were required to go to the blackboard and diagram complex sentences. Two or three years of Latin instruction helped to solidify the students' mastery of verb tenses, participial phrases, compound objects of prepositions, and the like. Writing skills were emphasized throughout the years of a student's education. It was only when I attended college and then law school that I realized how fortunate I was to have attended Brooklyn Friends.

Another feature of Brooklyn Heights life was the institution known as Miss Hepburn's Dance Class. Then in her eighties, Miss Hepburn had taught ballroom dancing to generations of Brooklyn Heights children since the turn of the century. Each fall, she would mail perfumed invitations to every student at four private schools: Brooklyn Friends, Poly Prep, Berkeley Carroll, and Carroll Gardens. Those who signed up would appear at 4:00 p.m. on Friday at Grace Church on Hicks Street. The boys would don their charcoal-gray suits and white gloves and were paired with female partners. One by one the couples would pass by Miss Hepburn, her pianist Miss Struthers, and the host chaperone of the day to say good afternoon and then be seated to await the beginning of the class. To get attention, Miss Hepburn would click a pair of castanets. Her instruction would then focus on the waltz, foxtrot, and, by popular demand, the Lindy. A small group of radicals persuaded Miss Hepburn to add the cha-cha to the curriculum.

Brooklyn Friends not only provided me with a first-class education but allowed me to excel in sports. I was captain of both the basketball and baseball teams—something I probably could not have achieved in a large public high school. My interest in sports led me to join the Grace Church Choir on Grace Court, which had a basketball court and a renowned choir led by well-known organist Anne McKittrick. With my soprano voice at age eleven, I shared the chancel with the Chapin brothers: Harry, Tom, and Steve. We all left the choir when our voices changed; however, Harry Chapin went on to pursue an illustrious career as a folk singer who had many top selling hits ("Taxi," "Cat's in the Cradle"). Years later, his life ended in a terrible accident on the Long Island Expressway.

Having an ecumenical bent, I left the Grace Church choir and, while still a student at the Quaker Brooklyn Friends School, I enrolled in the Garfield Temple Hebrew School to study for my bar mitzvah. There, I was instructed by Rabbi Eugene Sack, a towering figure in the Brooklyn Jewish community. My bar mitzvah "mate" was Eric Kaz, a Brooklyn Heights friend. When we weren't bike-riding, he would sometimes take out his guitar. He later moved to California and became a major songwriter, composing hits such as "Love Has No Pride" and "I Won't Be Hangin' 'Round" for Linda Ronstadt.

Forty-nine years later, as President of the Federal Bar Council, I was privileged to present to Rabbi Sack's son, the Honorable Robert Sack, the Council's Learned Hand Award. Judge Sack is a senior judge of the United States Court of Appeals for the Second Circuit. At the ceremony in the packed Grand Ballroom of the Waldorf-Astoria, I presented him with the signed prayer book that his late father had given me forty-nine years earlier on the occasion of my bar mitzvah. He was very moved by this surprise gesture, and it gave me great pleasure to have this opportunity.

Although the residents of Brooklyn Heights did not consider themselves part of Greater Brooklyn, they did share enthusiasm for the Brooklyn Dodgers. I would often visit the Dodgers' ticket office on Court Street and, on occasion, would take the BMT subway to Ebbets Field. My memories include watching Jackie Robinson steal home plate and seeing Duke Snider hit a home run over the 297-foot right-field fence onto Bedford Avenue, where boys would scramble for the ball.

At the Hotel Bossert, several of the Dodger players were housed for the season. One day, a local resident introduced me on the corner of Montague and Hicks Streets to Dodgers star pitcher Johnny Podres. I still have a picture of him with his arm around me; the top of my head barely reached his waist. 1955 was the year the Brooklyn Dodgers came into their own. With their first World Series victory, the streets around the Hotel Bossert were flooded with crowds cheering, shouting, and drinking in celebration of this world event.

A few years later, our Friends School class took a class trip to the Brooklyn docks, where we met the actor James Cagney, who was filming the movie *Never Steal Anything Small.* Whenever I come across that movie, in my mind's eye I can still see the docks where it was filmed.

CHAPTER 5

MY BEST FRIEND

In 1956, tabloid headlines shouted that playwright Arthur Miller had left his wife Mary and had gone off with actress Marilyn Monroe. The Miller family had lived for years in Brooklyn Heights in a brownstone at 155 Willow Street, where Arthur and Mary had raised two children: Bobby, a year younger than me, and Jane, a year older. I do not remember how we first met, but at the age of twelve or so, Bobby and I became fast friends. Practically every afternoon after school we would ride our bikes throughout the neighborhood, often racing down Squibb Hill at the end of Columbia Heights. We would frequently visit the famous Hotel St. George on Clark Street, which boasted the world's largest salt-water swimming pool. In the summer of 1960, my father took Bobby and me to a dude ranch in Putnam County, where we rode horses five hours a day. There were no televisions there. I remember that we listened on the radio to the heavyweight fight between Floyd Patterson and Ingemar Johansson.

In the fall of 1960, Bobby and I were walking on Fulton Street in downtown Brooklyn. As we approached Boerum Place,

Bobby spotted a crowd and pointed to a pickup truck. "Look, there's the man running for President of the United States," he said. We walked over and reached up to the back of the truck and shook hands with John F. Kennedy. The next summer, Bobby and I spent time in the sand hills of North Truro on Cape Cod, where Mary had rented a house for the summer.

When Mary and Arthur Miller divorced and Arthur married Marilyn Monroe, their custody agreement provided that Bobby and Jane would alternate their weekends—one with Mary in Brooklyn Heights and the other with Arthur and Marilyn, who divided their time between Sutton Place in Manhattan and their farm in Roxbury, Connecticut. Bobby and I would visit the Roxbury farm, where both Arthur and Marilyn could enjoy privacy, away from the tabloids and cameras. I recall that Arthur had a World War II–era jeep with a missing floorboard that he loved to drive around his property. Of course, as the world found out, the marriage did not last long; they separated in 1961, and in 1962, Marilyn died from an apparent overdose of sleeping pills.

Although Marilyn had no children of her own, she very much assumed the role of stepmother to Bobby and Jane. I recall having breakfast in the kitchen at the farm after Arthur and Marilyn separated. She called and spoke with Bobby. Although I could hear only Bobby's end of the conversation, it was clear that Marilyn was more like a mother than a world-famous actress.

Bobby's father, Arthur, had always supported liberal causes and was blacklisted as a result of the Communist hysteria during the McCarthy period. Bobby and his sister Jane attended the Little Red Schoolhouse and then Elisabeth Irwin High School in Greenwich Village, where children of many of the well-known "Left" were students. At some point, I learned a local secret: that one of the Meeropol boys (the children of Julius and Ethel

Rosenberg, who had been executed) was a student in Bobby's class. Some fifty years later, I saw a notice that one of the Meeropol sons, Robert, had written a new book entitled *An Execution in the Family* and was speaking at the local library in Larchmont, in Westchester County where I lived. I sat down with my son Daniel and gave him the short version of the Rosenberg spy case before taking him to the book signing at the library. At the end, I went up and introduced myself to Robert Meeropol and told him that I had grown up with Bobby Miller. He lit up at the recognition.

Bobby and I went down different paths after high school. While I went off to Union College in upstate New York, Bobby briefly attended his parents' alma mater at the University of Michigan but dropped out to become the road manager for the rock group the Lovin' Spoonful. Soon thereafter, he moved to the West Coast, and I saw him infrequently. In 2005 when Arthur Miller died, I saw an obituary that allowed me to track down Bobby in California. Soon thereafter, he came to New York with his college-aged daughter, Kate. I later hired her as a summer intern at my law firm before she pursued her own career.

From time to time, Bobby would call me for legal advice. Many years before his death, Arthur Miller had written a letter to the University of Texas expressing a desire to leave it the notes he made while he wrote *Death of a Salesman*. The university took the view that the letter gave it a right of first refusal—in other words, the right to match any other financial offer for the papers. However, over the years, Arthur had developed a good relationship with Yale, in Connecticut where Arthur lived. After Arthur died, Yale made a significant financial offer for the notes and the University of Texas matched it, demanding that its clamed right of first refusal be honored. From a financial perspective, it was a win/win for Arthur's estate. But the family was most concerned that the papers be properly displayed. The issue was particularly interesting, because each university had different kinds of displays in their centers for recognizing famous writers. And the laws of Connecticut and Texas were somewhat different on the issue of whether the qualitative nature of the displays could be considered in evaluating a matching offer, or only the financial aspect of the offer. The potential litigation was resolved with the notes sent to the University of Texas.

Years went by. In early 2022, I called Bob and asked him how he was doing. His response had the familiar friendly ring, but something did not quite sound right. "I guess I am doing okay," he said. Several months later, his daughter Kate called me and, in a voice conveying alarm, said, "Bob is not doing too well; we are very worried." A month or so later, Kate called again to tell me Bob had died. She asked if I would come to California and deliver remarks at a memorial gathering. I flew out to Laguna Beach to spend time with her and with Bob's half-sister, Rebecca, an accomplished producer in her own right, who is married to actor Daniel Day-Lewis. I was thankful for the opportunity to share with Rebecca and her husband many of the details of Bobby's early life. The actor seemed particularly taken by my recounting of the day Bobby and I had met John F. Kennedy standing on the back of a truck in Brooklyn.

CHAPTER 6
MY WORLD IS UPENDED

Life in our Brooklyn Heights home seemed to be, at least on the surface, fairly normal. Of course, I had nothing to compare it to. Typically, my parents would get home from work and have a martini about 6:00 p.m. before we had dinner, prepared by our live-in housekeeper. One evening in the spring of 1960, my father asked me to join my parents in the library room. He told me that my parents' marriage had reached a point where they wanted to have a trial separation. My mother would be leaving for an indefinite period of time to take up residence by herself in Manhattan. She said that she wanted to see me regularly for dinner—perhaps every week or two—and reassured me that this arrangement was fine with both of them. The next morning, I heard the center hall door close and looked out the window to see my mother walking down Remsen Street. I stuck my head out and said, "Mom, please come back." She turned around once, looked at me, and kept walking. She didn't turn back again.

Needless to say, I was quite upset when my mother left. I probed my father for the underlying reason but got no meaningful response. This unhappy development was particularly uncomfortable for me in my closely knit Friends School community and at summer camp, populated by many of the same students. At the time, separation and divorce were not the norm.

It was only several years later, in discussions with a woman with whom my father later had an affair, that I pieced together what had happened. I learned that the man in the raincoat who had beckoned to my mother on the stoop of our brownstone was a process server for the House Un-American Activities Committee, which in the late 1950s was still looking for Communists in every closet. Only by searching the internet in the last few years did I find out how that related to my mother. Apparently, this congressional Committee was investigating whether Communist influences had permeated the New York City Housing Authority—a favorite target of political conservatives—where my mother was the manager of a major housing project on the Lower East Side of Manhattan. I found my mother's testimony on the internet. She was apparently released by the Committee at the end of her appearance, with no further follow-up.

To deal with the congressional subpoena, my mother had contacted a nationally known lawyer, Telford Taylor, who had been a prosecutor assisting Justice Robert Jackson and later the lead American prosecutor at the post-war Nuremberg Trials. He was busy and recommended that my mother contact a colleague and well-known lawyer, Edward J. Ennis, who then represented her at the congressional hearing in 1958.

After that unhappy sit-down with my parents, I continued to live on Remsen Street with my father, largely focusing on my academics and athletics at the Friends School. I would see my mother on an irregular basis, looking forward to the steak dinner she would treat me to at a restaurant in Greenwich Village.

On each occasion, I would inquire what she was doing with her life, but I got only vague responses about her spending time with friends.

Two and a half years went by. I was a senior at Brooklyn Friends. One day, my father sat me down and said that he and my mother had decided to finalize their separation with a divorce. She was going to travel to Mexico, where this could be easily accomplished. By that time, I was not really surprised.

Several weeks later, my mother drove me home from one of our occasional dinners. She stopped the car to let me out in front of the house on Remsen Street, paused a moment, and turned to me and said, "I wanted you to know that when I went to Mexico to finalize the divorce, I also married Ed Ennis." She added that they had just purchased a summer house near the ocean in Lido Beach, Long Island, and she hoped I would be a frequent visitor. Completely taken by surprise, I felt a pit in my stomach. I said good night, went upstairs, and called my high-school girlfriend at the time to share the story. The feeling in my stomach did not go away quickly and reappeared each day for weeks thereafter.

As I later learned, Ed's representation of my mother before the House Un-American Activities Committee had blossomed into a covert affair, which my father had discovered when he happened to pick up the extension telephone in our house and overheard their conversation. This was the event that led to the sit-down when my father announced my parents' separation.

Edward Ennis had played an important part in our country's New Deal and World War II history. Born into a working-class Irish American family in Newark, New Jersey, in 1907, he graduated from Columbia Law School and secured a coveted clerkship with the Senior Circuit Judge of the United States Court of Appeals for the Second Circuit, Martin Thomas Manton.

(Manton was later indicted, tried, and convicted in a bribery scandal and resigned from office.) How Ed got that clerkship says a lot about how things worked in those days. Each year, Judge Manton would call the Dean of Columbia Law School and ask him to send him the brightest Catholic student in the graduating class. That was Ed.

Following his clerkship, Ed began a rapid ascension in the ranks of the Justice Department, holding positions as Chief of the Civil Division of the U.S. Attorney's Office for the Southern District of New York (based in Manhattan), and then a position as an Assistant Solicitor General in Washington, where he argued in defense of much of the New Deal legislation in the United States Supreme Court. Still a relatively young lawyer, he became a close counselor of Attorney General Francis Biddle. When Pearl Harbor was attacked on December 7, 1941, it was Ed who called the Attorney General that Sunday morning to advise him of the Japanese attack. Biddle asked him to draft the emergency legislation that became the blueprint for the internment of Japanese Americans living on the west coast. Biddle appointed him Director of Alien Enemy Control of the United States and he oversaw the entire Japanese internment program during World War II.

Much has been written about the internment program and Ed's role in it, including an important book by Professor Peter Irons, *Justice at War: The Story of the Japanese-American Internment Cases*, published in 1993. What much of the public did not know until much later was that Ed fought internally within the government to address the misleading statements by top leaders in the government and the military about the dangers that Japanese Americans supposedly posed. The leading cases of the United States Supreme Court that upheld the constitutionality of the Japanese internment program were *Hirabayashi v. United States*, decided in 1943, and *Korematsu v. United States*, decided in 1944. Ed oversaw the drafting of the Justice Department's briefs to the U.S. Supreme Court, objecting to statements in the brief that said there was evidence of Japanese Americans signaling with lights to ships from the west coast. Ed sought to include a footnote in the *Korematsu* brief disavowing the claims of espionage, but was overruled by, among others, John J. McCloy, the Assistant Secretary of War.

In the 1980s, Hirabayashi and Korematsu brought *coram nobis* proceedings in federal court, seeking to use new evidence to overturn their wartime convictions that had been upheld by the Supreme Court based on the government's brief. Then eighty years of age, Ed testified as a witness in the proceedings to support them, after their lawyers had used the Freedom of Information Act to obtain a copy of Ed's internal memorandum protesting the statements in the government's brief. Ed also testified before Congress to support reparations for those Americans of Japanese ancestry who were interned during the war. Several years ago, former Acting Solicitor General Neal Katyal, in a speech at NYU Law School, issued a confession of error by the Justice Department based on Ed's internal memorandum. A few years ago, I gave an interview for a documentary that chronicled these events.

After the war, Ed left the Department of Justice and had an unusual career in both private practice and in the *pro bono* world. He was recruited by the Japanese American Citizens League to recover property that the government had seized during the war—a legal action that did not succeed. He was retained by Fritz von Opel to try to recover the U.S. assets of his Opel automobile company. And the American Civil Liberties Union reached out to Ed, which led to decades of *pro bono* service for that organization. He served as its General Counsel for many years and later as the Chairman of the Board. Each year at the group's annual meeting in New York, the heads of each regional chapter would come to the house for dinner and discuss the leading civil liberties cases they were involved in throughout the United States.

In later years, the American Civil Liberties Union called upon Ed to argue in the U.S. Supreme Court some of their most important cases. One of these was *Afroyim v. Rusk*, a case that established that one does not lose United States citizenship by voting in a foreign election, and that there must be a voluntary renunciation. When I was in law school, I sat in the gallery at the Supreme Court to watch Ed argue *Walz v. Tax Commission*, in which the plaintiff challenged the tax exemption in New York for church-owned property. The case was a predictable loser, although the decision dismissing it drew a dissent from Justice William O. Douglas. Although there were strong arguments that the tax exemption in New York City violated the Establishment Clause of the First Amendment, the Court clearly was not ready to disturb customs that had been in place for hundreds of years.

During this postwar period, my stepfather had no shortage of interesting clients in private practice. One of these, an Indian businessman named Jayanti Dharma Teja, is discussed later in this book. Others included Serge Rubinstein, a flamboyant entrepreneur whom the Department of Justice prosecuted during World War II under Ed's supervision. He later retained Ed as his personal lawyer. One morning, newspaper headlines blared that Rubinstein had been found murdered in his Fifth Avenue New York City townhouse. Under his will, my stepfather was named as trustee for his two daughters who had not yet reached adulthood. The trustee service continued for many years thereafter. In an unrelated matter, Ed served as coexecutor for his client Gilbert Heublein, the liquor magnate, who died at a relatively young age, leaving a large fortune. When I asked how a lifetime litigator became a successful trusts-and-estates lawyer, Ed responded, "It's by the happenstance of outliving your peers." It occurred to me that quite apart from professional reasons, that is something worth hoping for.

Over many decades, I developed a close relationship with Ed, while maintaining my relationship with my father, Jerome. In the late 1970s, Ed and I would go out west each year and ski in the Rockies. I had free use of the summer home in Lido Beach, as well as the townhouse near Park Avenue in Manhattan, particularly when my mother and Ed were traveling, which they did for weeks at a time. Over the course of several years, they provided me with a series of top-end sports cars, beginning with a Triumph TR4; a Jaguar XK-E; and finally, a lightly used Mercedes-Benz 300SL sports car, then one of the world's premier luxury sportscars. While any young person in my position would have been thrilled with this apparent generosity, I know full well that my mother carried with her a deep sense of guilt for having abandoned me at age nine months and then again at age fourteen. By the time I reached my mid-twenties, I had pretty much lost my interest not only in cars, but in material things generally. Living at my own apartment on the Upper East Side of Manhattan, I was happy to travel by subway, taxi, or Hertz rental car whenever I needed transportation.

CHAPTER 7

OFF TO COLLEGE

In the fall of 1963, I entered Union College in upstate New York. Like many small colleges, it was single-sex; coeducation in these colleges did not happen until a decade later. I had never seriously considered any other college, as two older boys I knew had raved about their experiences there. Although Union had only 1,800 students, for some time I felt a bit lost, having spent most of my life in the small Brooklyn Friends school. While following the usual path into fraternity life, I developed an intense interest in radio broadcasting and trained myself to mimic the then-popular rock-and-roll DJ presentation, practicing it for over a year on the college radio station. I progressed rather swiftly. One day, the head of our college station, Dick Ferguson, got a phone call from the program director of a major 50,000-watt AM radio station in Albany, WPTR, that had a problem on its hands. (In those days, FM radio stations were few and far between, and a handful of 50,000-watt AM "giants," whose broadcasts at night could be heard throughout much of the country, ruled the roost.) The all-night disc jockey had been fired, and they needed a temporary replacement. Ferguson recommended me as a fill-in, and I rushed to the station for an audition, which resulted in my hosting the midnight-to-6:00 a.m. slot for six consecutive nights, until a permanent replacement could be found.

Leaping from the college radio station to a 50,000-watt radio giant was a heady experience for a twenty-year-old. In those days, teenagers did not have Facebook or TikTok to occupy themselves. Rock-and-roll radio was their primary form of entertainment 24/7. Our studio was constantly besieged with phone calls, and groups of teenagers would occasionally greet me as I exited the studio. With my foot in the door, I spent the month filling in at WPTR and was then sent to the radio equivalent of a baseball "farm club" in Kingston, New York, where I hosted a daily afternoon radio station for the remainder of the summer of 1966. When I returned to Union in the fall, I was offered a permanent slot on Saturday night and Sunday at WPTR's competitor WTRY, where I worked until graduation from college the following spring. Although I had applied and had been accepted to law school, I was considering deferring my legal education because WOR-FM in New York (later renamed WCBS-FM) was introducing a rock-and-roll format, and I was a candidate for a slot, because the program director had heard my show on a New Haven, Connecticut, radio show. However, the Vietnam war was raging, and that summer, I received my Greetings from the President, who ordered me to report to Fort Hamilton in Brooklyn for a physical examination. Suddenly, the prospect of law school with a temporary educational deferment seemed ideal; rock-and-roll disc jockeys were not on the deferred list.

During two summers between years at college, I managed to pursue one of my dreams—motorcycling in Europe. On both trips, I traveled with a college friend, Paul. I first befriended him by happenstance on a charter flight to Amsterdam. I knew him vaguely from Union but had not spoken to him before that flight. My mother had encouraged me to visit Europe on the condition that I enroll in a university in Grenoble, France, to improve my primitive French. Neither my parents nor I had made any prior arrangements for this venture. It was up to me to find my way to the university and enroll. On the plane to Amsterdam, my new friend Paul told me that he planned to purchase a used Volkswagen and make his way to Italy, where he would board a ferry from Brindisi for Greece to visit a friend who had been an exchange student at Union.

It took twenty-four hours to reach Amsterdam in a prop plane that stopped in Gander, Newfoundland, and Reykjavik, Iceland, with some attendant engine problems along the way. By the time we got to Amsterdam, I had persuaded Paul to abandon the idea of purchasing a Volkswagen and instead joining me in purchasing a motorcycle. In Amsterdam, we soon found a motorcycle store and purchased two identical motorcycles. We traveled on secondary roads to Paris, where we checked into the Hotel California, a small hotel on the Left Bank. Sitting down for continental breakfast in the small hotel lobby, Paul and I encountered three college-age young women from Sweden who were sharing a room above ours. Before long, Paul had gone off on his motorcycle with one of them—a young woman named Sigrid—and, as often happens at that age, romance was in the air. We had planned to go our separate ways immediately upon reaching Paris—Paul toward Greece and me toward southern France—but he wanted to stay another week in Paris to spend time with his new companion. I accommodated our friendship and, at the same time, warded off a sense of guilt for not going to Grenoble by remaining in Paris and enrolling in the Alliance Française, a language school for foreigners.

Eventually, the three Swedish girls returned home, and Paul and I continued our motorcycle journey through France to the French Riviera, where we visited an Indian client of Ed's at his enormous villa in Cannes, overlooking the Mediterranean. More on this later. Eventually, we parted company in Nice. I put my motorcycle on a train and went back to Paris and assumed Paul had gone on to Greece. Before separating, we agreed to meet at the end of the summer at a certain time and place in London on a designated street corner. This was decades before the advent of cellphones.

Back in Paris, I met a young lady from Minnesota who had just purchased a sports car, which provided me with transportation for the remainder of my stay in exchange for providing her with a place to stay. I then negotiated the sale of my motorcycle at a Paris train station, where I boarded a train for Amsterdam to return to the small hotel where I had left most of my luggage before purchasing my motorcycle. Retrieving my luggage, I took a taxi to the airport to fly to London to meet Paul at the appointed time and place on a street corner.

At the agreed-upon hour, sure enough, Paul showed up on the London street corner and we enjoyed a big hug. "How was Greece?" I asked him. He responded that he never got there. Instead, when he had reached Rome, he had been overcome with lovesickness and booked an airplane to Sweden to visit and travel for several days with his new Swedish love, Sigrid. After spending several days in London, we returned to New York. Quite an adventurous summer for two nineteen-year-old college students.

Two summers later, Paul and I wanted to repeat the adventure but with an upgrade on our motorcycles. Paul had been corresponding by mail with Sigrid over the last two years, and more than anything, he wanted to visit her again in Sweden. I was happy to make the trip with him to the Nordic countries. We pulled out a map and decided we would fly to London and try to purchase Triumph or BSA motorcycles, the pride of the UK fleet. When we got there, we found we would have to pay a huge 50 percent tax, so that seemed to make little sense. We pulled out the map again and put a pencil down on Hamburg, Germany, which seemed to be a good launching point for Denmark and ultimately Sweden. We boarded an overnight train from London to Belgium and arrived in the morning in Hamburg, Germany. We asked for directions to the closest motorcycle dealer, where we saw two identical used BMW R26 motorcycles in the window. We walked in, put down our travelers' checks, and completed the purchases by noon. The proprietor was so thrilled that he sent his son with us to the local motor vehicle bureau to register the motorcycles in our names. By 3:00 p.m., we were headed north on a beautiful sunny afternoon, with grass fields on either side of a country road, headed for Denmark and ultimately reached Copenhagen. The next day, we headed to the port in Denmark for the ferry that would take us to Malmö at the southern tip of Sweden. On the ferry, we camped out on the deck and made friends with a couple of students who were on their own adventure. We traded stories and exchanged addresses.

Arriving in Sweden, we motored up the coast to the beach town Tylösand, where Paul's motorcycle got some repairs. We finally reached Stockholm, where we checked into student dorms at the university. I planned to wait there for the big event, Paul's reunion with Sigrid ninety miles north of Stockholm. While there, I tooled around on my motorcycle, soon making friends with a female American college student attending the University of California, Davis. We rode around for two days exploring the city and sampled the nightlife in the underground bars. It was nice to have companionship in a country so far from home. On the third or fourth day, Paul returned, and immediately I knew something was wrong. Paul had found Sigrid in a local hospital, where she was recovering from an abortion. Whatever happened between the two of them, I never asked about it. Sadly, Paul's two-year-long fantasy had evaporated.

From Stockholm, we motored south. Reaching the southern tip of Sweden, we put our motorcycles on a ferry that docked in northern Germany. We unloaded our motorcycles at dawn and were met with beautiful, sunny July weather as we traveled the country roads south, stopping in Stuttgart, Germany. From there we continued south to Lucerne, Switzerland, where we met two college girls who hitched a ride with us to the chairlift to Mount Pilatus, which provided beautiful views of the Swiss countryside. We heard cowbells in the distance. It felt like we were in a TV advertisement for Swiss cheese. In my mind's eye, I could picture a young Swiss girl wearing a colorful apron and churning a barrel of milk.

The next day we continued our journey south through rush-hour traffic in Milan and Genoa, passed through Monte Carlo, and headed for the villa in Cannes that we had visited two summers before. Ed's Indian client, Jayanti Dharma Teja, who owned the villa, had become wealthy with a franchise to develop India's merchant-marine fleet, with the blessing of the Nehru government. My stepfather, Ed, as his lawyer, had helped Teja navigate the process. Apparently, the change in the Indian government led to a criminal investigation of Teja. He owed Ed very substantial legal fees. In partial satisfaction of that obligation, Teja had signed over to Ed the Cannes villa, as well as two Mercedes-Benz 300 SL sports cars that were garaged there. Before I left for this summer trip, my mother and Ed had asked me to stop by there to check things out. This time, things were very different, because Ed was now the new owner.

It is difficult to describe this villa. Set on a hill overlooking the Mediterranean, it was shaped as a long building with two wings on either side. I didn't count the number of rooms, but it was surely more than twenty. When Paul and I arrived, we pulled up full of soot and road dust, surprising a group of four servants living there and two American girls, our age, who were friends of Teja's wife. We announced ourselves, and although things seemed a bit awkward, because the staff was unaware of the details of the transfer of the property to my stepfather, we were well-treated and spent a week with our newly found college friends, exploring the area on our motorcycles and sunning on the beach in Cannes.

When we began to feel restless, Paul and I continued our journey along the Gold Coast, arriving in Barcelona, Spain. Eventually, we drove north through Andorra and the Pyrenees mountains, then back to Paris. There, we arranged to drive our motorcycles to the port of Le Havre, to be shipped back to New York, where we soon returned.

The summer of 1967 came to an end in late August. I remember meeting my mother soon thereafter, in New York. She handed me an envelope, telling me she had not wanted to interfere with my summer enjoyment. It was my Greetings from the President ordering me to appear at Fort Hamilton for a physical exam. But because I was about to enter law school, it was postponed as I was temporarily deferred as a student.

The passage of many decades has given me a much better understanding of who I was during my four years at Union College. Most of us are very different people at age seventeen or eighteen when entering college than we are four years later. And I have come to realize that at age twenty-one, most women are far ahead of men in the path to adulthood.

Young people today would find it hard to imagine what college social life was like sixty years ago. At a typical men's college, socializing with young women was confined to the weekends, when fraternity brothers would host dates at beer parties in the basement of the fraternity house or cocktail parties after a Saturday home football game. Many of the young women would be looking to tie down a permanent relationship by graduation day. Not so the men. In fact, freshmen men had virtually no chance to develop a social life—hence the attraction of fraternities, which offered a place to entertain as well as transportation afforded by upper-class "brothers" with cars. But for first-semester men, the social life was cramped to say the least. On occasion at an appointed hour, a bus would appear in a dorm parking lot with about forty young women from a nearby women's college. The men would assemble and wait for the women to emerge, one by one. What followed was some not-so-subtle maneuvering by the men, each seeking to begin a conversation with an attractive young lady. Once people were paired up, the only place they had to go for conversation was a local bar, as women were absolutely forbidden to enter college dorms.

My own immaturity is best illustrated by my relationship with my college girlfriend. In my senior year, one Saturday evening we were parked on a bluff overlooking the Hudson River. She turned to me and asked, "Mark, where are we going?" I responded, "I'm going to the studio to do my radio show." Looking back, I realize how insensitive this was. Perhaps more importantly, it made clear how we were in different universes. In fact, it was another twenty years before I would marry. That was a relationship that lasted for twenty-two more years, but unfortunately did not survive.

CHAPTER 8
LAW SCHOOL

The first year of law school comes as a jolt to many recent college graduates. In the 1960s, college students generally enjoyed a welcoming and embracing environment. But law schools were known for their rigid classroom style and demanding curriculum, attended by relatively formal interchanges between professors and students. The atmosphere was best exemplified (if somewhat exaggerated) by actor John Houseman portraying Harvard Professor Kingsfield in the popular movie and television series *The Paper Chase*.

NYU Law School was at least a little bit different. Situated in Greenwich Village on the legendary Washington Square Park, the law school environment seemed to reflect some of the liberal politics and personal behavior represented by hippie life, political demonstrators, and pot smokers who seemed to call Washington Square Park their own (my first week attending law school was the first time I smelled the aroma of marijuana).

But make no mistake about it. The hard reality was that law school was not the kinder, gentler Union College. There, as a political science major, you could expect to enjoy a beer from time to time with one of your professors in the underground Rathskeller. Not so at NYU on Washington Square. Professors were all business. They would leave class and disappear, letting you know that if you had a question about the subject matter, you could make an appointment during their office hours. But if you secured that opportunity, you didn't expect to share your experiences motorcycling in Europe, working as an all-night disc jockey, or struggling with the draft board. Unless you were an attractive female student, your professor would probably have no interest in such subjects. The environment was like cold water in my face. It made me realize that I had to leave my old life behind, because nobody but me cared about it.

On top of the usual academic pressures that students experienced, in that year and several that followed we witnessed monumental events that affected law students as well as the nation at large. In the spring of 1968, Martin Luther King was assassinated. In June, while studying for final exams, we learned that Robert F. Kennedy had been murdered. In early 1968, President Johnson had announced that student deferments would end for all first-year law students, making them subject to immediate draft for service in Vietnam. Many of the students in my class were strongly opposed to the war. Of course, the views and motivations varied widely: some were willing to serve, but sought out reserve units, making service in Vietnam less likely; others, morally opposed to serving in any capacity, left law school and fled to Canada, giving up their U.S. citizenship. I did not see some of these classmates until class reunions years later after President Jimmy Carter had granted them clemency.

Although opposed to the war, I had mixed feelings about my own military service. At one point, I learned that there were a few openings at NYU for a two-year ROTC officer's program that would allow me to complete law school. Along with several dozen other competing students, I showed up on a Saturday morning to take a written test. It had two parts: a verbal section that consisted of multiple-choice questions that most sixth graders could answer correctly, and a mechanical section. As I recall, this consisted of a picture of something like a worm gear and pictures of several other items I did not recognize. We were supposed to choose the match. I never was told my score. I assume I correctly answered every question in the verbal section and got every answer wrong in the mechanical section, so my overall score was probably 50 percent. No wonder I wasn't selected.

Eventually, I chose a route sanctioned by the draft board and encouraged by New York City, throwing my lot in with others to teach elementary school in a disadvantaged neighborhood in Brooklyn. I did that for several months, then decided to resign and take my chances with the draft. I told the draft board I was available, and it quickly obliged. Fort Hamilton was then the next stop. "You're going to 'Nam, boy," one soldier shouted to me. You can picture in your mind's eye one hundred young men standing in their underwear in a large room, lined up as in the immigration reception at JFK Airport, to be interviewed briefly by one of a dozen doctors sitting at kiosks. Afterward, I didn't hear anything from the draft board. A short time later, the draft was changed to a lottery system based on one's birthdate. I was never called and I returned to law school.

On March 6, 1970, during my second year in law school, a huge explosion demolished a townhouse on West 11th Street in Greenwich Village. Three members of the Weather Underground (known as Weathermen), a radical leftist group, were killed. Two survivors, Kathy Boudin and Cathy Wilkerson, escaped and fled.

The townhouse was being used as a major bomb factory, where the conspirators were planning to blow up, among other sites, an event at Fort Dix in New Jersey and the Administration Building at Columbia University. Boudin and Wilkerson had already been charged with assault in Chicago and forfeited their bail. In New York, they were charged with unlawful possession of dynamite. The two were placed on the FBI's Ten Most Wanted Fugitives list for more than a decade. Wilkerson surrendered in 1980 and Boudin was captured a year later, having participated in the 1981 Brink's armored-car robbery in which three people were murdered. She was in prison until released in 2003 and was later hired as an adjunct professor at Columbia.

Kathy Boudin was the daughter of a famed civil liberties lawyer, Leonard Boudin. Kathy's brother, the late Michael Boudin, was a distinguished lawyer, and served as the Chief Judge of the United States Court of Appeals for the First Circuit. Kathy's son, Chesa Boudin, was the District Attorney in San Franscico; he was recalled from office in 2022.

Two days after the townhouse bombing, I visited my mother and stepfather Ed at their townhouse off Park Avenue. Invited there for dinner was Kathy's father, Leonard Boudin, who appeared exhausted from the trauma that had just occurred, with his daughter now a fugitive. After dinner, I left the house and got in my parked car. As I pulled away, I noticed a car behind me turn on its headlights. Given the events that had just occurred, in a moment of paranoia I wondered if I was being followed. To test out my fear, I turned at the next corner and made a series of turns until I returned to my original parking spot. Sure enough, the car was still behind me. I then started up again, this time heading for the FDR Drive to go to Brooklyn. At some point, whoever was following me either lost me or lost interest in me.

Upon reflection, I assumed that law enforcement had been following Leonard Boudin on the possibility that either he or someone on his behalf would lead them to his fugitive daughter.

When many of us had returned to law school after a year's absence, the national trauma only continued. In the spring of 1970, President Richard Nixon ordered the invasion of Cambodia, causing a national firestorm. In May 1970, students at Kent State University were shot by national guardsmen who were tasked with curbing demonstrations there. The incident brought into sharp relief the country's divisions and agony over the conduct of the Vietnam War. Immediately after the Cambodia invasion, many of the students and NYU law professors organized to take chartered buses to Washington to meet with congressmen to voice objection to the Vietnam war. My group met with Ed Koch—then serving as a Representative from New York, before his days as Mayor of the City.

Entering my third and final year in law school, I found myself behind my fellow students in thinking about the future. While some were just finding their footing after returning from military service or alternative pursuits during the Vietnam War, others were clearly focused on "the money," signing up for interviews on campus with Wall Street law-firm recruiters. This route became particularly attractive later that year when Cravath, a Wall Street law firm, raised its starting salary from $10,000 to $15,000, a 50 percent increase. Perhaps because I had little interest in that route, I missed the deadlines for those interviews.

During the summer of 1970, before my final year, I had been privileged to secure an internship in the Criminal Division of the U.S. Attorney's office for the Southern District of New York. It was exciting to accompany skilled lawyers trying cases and arguing appeals. As I entered my final year at law school, it became clear to me that I wanted to be a litigator.

One of the most useful and prestigious paths a law-school graduate can follow is serving a year or two as a clerk for a federal judge. Today, each year federal judges receive hundreds of applications from aspiring graduates, generally leaving it to their law clerks to sort through the stacks of resumes and send all but a few applicants a form rejection letter. In 1970, the legal world, like the rest of the country, seemed a little more personal. In those days, if you had a question about your utility service or the railroad schedule, you could pick up the telephone and speak with a human after a few rings.

Not knowing exactly how to begin securing a clerkship, I visited the law-school library, took from the shelf one of the books with published federal court cases, and opened to the part that listed the names of every federal district judge. For someone who plans to be a litigator, these trial-level clerkships are perhaps the most useful, although some would prefer seeking a clerkship with a circuit court of appeals or the most prestigious ones at the United States Supreme Court, which ironically is probably less useful for the future trial lawyer.

I decided to write a letter to every district judge in Manhattan, Brooklyn, Connecticut, and New Jersey, attaching my resume and a letter of recommendation I had received from Whitney North Seymour, Jr., the United States Attorney for the Southern District of New York, the office where I had interned during the summer. Seymour was particularly gracious in providing this support for those who had interned in the office.

Somewhat to my surprise, I received personal letters from every single judge to whom I had written (I recall there were well over twenty of them). Many actually apologized, saying that their clerks had already been chosen. Some wished me good luck in my legal career. Three judges invited me for an interview. The first chambers I called were those of Judge Robert Shaw in Newark, New Jersey (Newark would be a relatively quick commute from my apartment in Brooklyn Heights: five minutes on the subway to the newly built World Trade Center, and then a fifteen-minute PATH ride to downtown Newark). I showed up at the scheduled time to meet Judge Shaw, who spent a few minutes questioning me then said, "You've got the job. It will be a GS-9 level position that pays ninety-five hundred dollars a year." I thanked him and he said, "Show up on August fifteenth."

Before the date of the scheduled interview with Judge Shaw, I had visited the NYU Law School Placement Office, which was supposed to assist students in finding jobs, particularly coveted clerkships. I told the woman in charge that I had an interview scheduled with Judge Shaw and asked for a letter of recommendation. She looked at her card catalog and said, "I see we have already recommended two students to this judge and they did not receive any responses. We are not going to recommend a third." When I returned from the interview with Judge Shaw, I stopped into the Placement Office and saw the same woman. I told her that I got the job. She blurted out, "You did?" I told her yes, but no thanks to her. Thank you, NYU Law School.

PART TWO

THE JOURNEY

CHAPTER 9

CLERKING IN THE FEDERAL COURT

Showing up on my first day of work at Judge Shaw's chambers was exciting. Although I had not yet received the results of the bar exam, it was my first day working as a real lawyer. I carried with me the idealism that had been fired up in me by several of the excellent law professors at the law school, particularly the concepts of due process and justice. However, my idealism was soon tempered by reality. My first surprise was to learn that my first duty was to make coffee for the judge, his secretary, and the judge's assigned court stenographer. Fortunately, and more substantively, two experiences stand out in my mind that illustrate the chasm between idealism and the real world.

One of the matters before Judge Shaw was a civil-rights case entitled *Lewis v. Kugler* (the latter party was the Chief of the New Jersey State Police). Known as the Long-Haired Travelers case, this civil-rights lawsuit claimed the state police were routinely stopping on the New Jersey Turnpike drivers who had long hair.

According to the complaint, the pretextual police stops were used as an excuse for searching for drugs. Judge Shaw had dismissed the case, but the United States Court of Appeals for the Third Circuit reversed and remanded the matter for Judge Shaw to hear testimony, which took place at the beginning of my clerkship. I watched the lawyers for the State trying to defend the conduct of the police. To his credit, Judge Shaw, a conservative Democrat who probably despised long hair, was offended by the testimony he heard and accordingly issued an injunction against the challenged conduct, which the Third Circuit Court of Appeals later affirmed. It made a big impression on me.

The second event that stands out took place at the beginning of my clerkship. One of the outgoing clerks was assigned to orient me in my duties. At one point, we passed a large bookcase full of legal files. The clerk said, "These are habeas corpus petitions for you to review when you have time, but don't make them a priority." What I had learned in law school was that habeas corpus—known in England as the "Great Writ"—was a bedrock concept in jurisprudence that enables courts to bring a person from custody, requiring authorities to explain themselves. I wondered why these petitions should be such a low priority.

Immersing myself in my job, I went into the deserted chambers on a weekend and started to review the habeas petitions, almost all of them from state prisoners who claimed that some sort of constitutional violation was responsible for their incarceration. The first thing I noticed was that the State, represented by the Attorney General's office, had not responded to the petitions, even though many of them had been pending for months, if not more than a year. On Monday, I reported this to Judge Shaw. He raised his eyebrows, looked at me, and said, "Call the Attorney

General himself and tell him if he doesn't respond to these petitions promptly, I will turn all these people loose."

Duly charged with this task, I called the Attorney General's office and said that I was calling at the direction of a federal judge who told me to speak to the Attorney General. Sure enough, the Attorney General came to the phone and I delivered Judge Shaw's message. The next week, Judge Shaw's chambers were flooded with briefs responding to all the petitions.

Among the many petitions for habeas relief, one of them caught my eye. In 1967, Plainfield, New Jersey, had experienced riots in which a police officer was killed and several people were injured. One man and one woman had been tried and convicted of murder in New Jersey Superior Court and were sentenced to life imprisonment by a jury, which at the time had the option to impose a death sentence, but did not. The New Jersey Appellate Division reversed the conviction, and the State had taken an appeal to the New Jersey Supreme Court, which would ultimately make the choice of either affirming the trial court conviction, or alternatively affirming the Appellate Division's reversal of the conviction, which would lead to a retrial. However, in the event of a retrial, under prevailing New Jersey law, since the jury in the first trial had opted for life imprisonment rather than the death penalty, a conviction at a new trial could no longer result in the death penalty being imposed, because this would no longer be a "capital case," for which bail could be denied. Bail would therefore be a right under New Jersey law. With the case in this posture on appeal, the defendants, represented by Rutgers Law Professor Frank Askin, asked the New Jersey Superior Court to grant bail pending the state's appeal, which they argued was a matter of right in a case that was no longer a capital case. The motion was summarily denied, and both the Appellate Division and the New Jersey Supreme Court declined to intervene.

After I reviewed the history of these proceedings, it was obvious to me that the defendants were entitled to bail, but none of the state judges at any level who reviewed this matter apparently understood this—or perhaps even cared to think about it. I prepared a memorandum for Judge Shaw summarizing the situation and recommending that he order the prisoners to be released on bail. Judge Shaw at first was skeptical, but after reviewing my memorandum and the cases I cited, he agreed with me. I had enormous respect for him. As a relatively conservative former town politician, Judge Shaw must not have been eager to free these people. But he instructed me to call a hearing, and at the conclusion, he ordered the State of New Jersey to grant the defendants bail. The case is *United States ex rel. Merritt v. Vukcevich*, 339 F. Supp. 779 (D.N.J. 1972).

This case, perhaps unimportant in the larger scheme of things, was troubling to me. How is it that conscientious judges in the New Jersey state system could fail to do their duty when the correct course was so clear to me, a first-year lawyer, and ultimately to Judge Shaw? I could only assume this situation, by extrapolation, must occur thousands of times a year in our judicial system. It is far from perfect.

CHAPTER 10
MOVING ON

Like all federal judges' clerks, I would routinely receive invitations from law firms to interview with them. I saved these letters but never responded to them. Midway through my clerkship, Judge James Rosen, a judge on the Third Circuit Court of Appeals that sat in Philadelphia, extended me an offer to clerk for him for a year on the Circuit Court after I finished my year with Judge Shaw. I was hesitant, thinking that an appellate clerkship would be far less interesting than being in the trenches of litigation warfare in the District Court. While service as a clerk for a judge on the Circuit Court is certainly prestigious and of interest to many, it is generally not regarded as an exciting place to be. Many district judges have no interest in being appointed to that court, because they would be deprived of the day-to-day contact with lawyers that many enjoy in the District Court. One friend of mine, a judge on the Court of Appeals for the Second Circuit, once commented to me, "The most exciting thing that happens each day is that the mail arrives." Soon, a fortuitous event occurred that pointed me in a new direction.

The Ballantine Beer Brewery in Newark was a long-standing institution that employed many workers in this industrial city. Longtime Yankees fans will recall the television ads in the 1950s that began, "Hey, get your cold beer." The Falstaff Brewing Company made a deal to purchase Ballantine, which certain labor unions objected to, claiming the deal would violate their contractual rights. The week before the planned closing, the unions brought an action before Judge Shaw seeking an injunction and a temporary restraining order to stop the acquisition. An emergency hearing was held on a Friday afternoon. Judge Shaw heard argument and at the conclusion, denied the temporary restraining order and then left for the day. A horde of lawyers for Falstaff and the unions came to the judge's chambers, where my co-clerk and I had to negotiate with the lawyers and draft a form of judicial order to embody the judge's ruling. This would allow the losing party to seek out a judge of the Court of Appeals on Saturday morning to request a restraining order, as the deal was slated to close on Monday. When the form of order was prepared and agreed to by the lawyers, my co-clerk had to drive to the judge's home to have it signed and then filed back in Newark.

The matter was settled early the following week. A few days later, I received a telephone call from the lead lawyer who had represented Falstaff, a senior partner at the Manhattan law firm known as Kaye, Scholer, Fierman, Hays & Handler. Actually, the call was placed by his secretary—a formal but usual way of communicating that I had not yet experienced. The partner said he had been impressed with me and invited me for an interview. I showed up on a Friday afternoon, was interviewed and taken to lunch by several lawyers, and extended an offer on Monday morning. I accepted on the spot. Looking back, I probably did so not just because the firm had a fine reputation, but because at the time, I wanted to get back to New York.

CHAPTER 11

LEARNING TO BE A TRIAL LAWYER

Sitting in Judge Shaw's chambers in Newark, I would often pick up the *New York Law Journal*, which was delivered daily. I saw that a new organization was being formed: the National Institute for Trial Advocacy (NITA) was organizing at the University of Colorado a one-month training course for aspiring trial lawyers. The program would feature instructors who were judges and leading trial lawyers from around the country. The tuition for a full month in August was one hundred dollars, all in. Even at what the dollar was worth then, it seemed like a great deal, and I signed up.

In order to attend the program, I had to use my four weeks of allotted vacation at the tail end of my clerkship. Today, in my experience, few lawyers choose to spend their vacation taking professional training. Recreational travel, sometimes to exotic places, seems to be much higher on the list. Perhaps lawyers today have a better sense of work-life balance. But at the time, with the experience behind me as an intern and law clerk, I was hell-bent on learning to try cases.

In early August, I started out on a Friday evening from Brooklyn Heights, working my way through rush-hour traffic in New Jersey and driving all night through a monumental rainstorm that flooded eastern Pennsylvania. I pulled over to the side of the road Saturday morning at about 4:00 a.m. in eastern Ohio to catch a nap. At some point, I was awakened by a bright light shining in my eyes. It was a police officer knocking on my window to inquire what I was doing there. Since he apparently did not think I was a wanted felon, he left, and I began another long day of driving until I passed through Chicago and checked into a Holiday Inn at about 7:00 p.m. on Saturday night in Davenport, Iowa. I gulped down a couple of shots of scotch and a hamburger, fell into my bed, and arose to continue the journey at 7:00 a.m. I drove all day through Iowa and Nebraska (the road was so straight you could practically take your hands off the wheel for minutes at a time) and finally turned southwest for Boulder, Colorado. With the benefit of a two-hour time difference from New York, I arrived at the University of Colorado, left my luggage in a dorm, and showed up for the opening session of the NITA program at 6:00 p.m. on Sunday.

The month-long trial skills program was the highlight of my professional life thus far. Each day, for a month, we were given the opportunity to practice trial presentations, every morning, afternoon, and evening, seven days a week. We would receive instruction and critiques from our tutors, working our way through the many mistakes that new lawyers make. By the end of the program, as I later found out, I probably had gained more trial experience, even in this mock setting, than most of my peers in a decade or more of practice in a major law firm. These were skills that significantly advantaged me in the years to come.

CHAPTER 12

PRIVATE PRACTICE

Kaye Scholer was a new experience for me. The law firm had an excellent reputation and placed a heavy emphasis on lawyer training. As is the case at all large law firms, the path of a new associate was highly regimented. First-year associates were assigned to share a windowed office with another lawyer. Given credit for my year of service as a judicial law clerk, I qualified as a second-year lawyer and was accorded entry into the next tier: a solo interior office with no window. The standard furniture arrangement consisted of a desk with a telephone, two small chairs, and a dictating machine with a three-inch belt to record dictation, which I had never tried. As a law clerk, I had been assigned a Royal mechanical typewriter while my co-clerk had the use of an electric typewriter. At my new firm, an associate lawyer had the option of either dictating into the machine and dropping the belt off at a central "steno pool" or calling down to the pool supervisor and requesting that a stenographer come to the lawyer's office to take live dictation. I tried both. As it turned out, learning to dictate, whether to a machine or live person, was the most important skill I could master. To this day, after more than fifty years, I dictate every memorandum or brief, allowing me to keep up with my thoughts without struggling to write or type—neither of which I ever did very well.

If an associate was still in good standing by the third year, he or she was provided the luxury of a solo, windowed office and the services of a personal secretary, shared with one other lawyer. The secretary operated an IBM Selectric electric typewriter and was skilled in cutting and pasting as the lawyer revised drafts of memos and briefs. In the fourth year, if you survived that long, the ultimate luxury was provided. Added to the lawyer's tools were a speakerphone (an item that conveyed prestige) and the services of a secretary assigned only to you. At the time, word processing was in its infancy. The steno pool had a computer installation, crude by today's standards, that allowed storage of boilerplate documents such as wills and corporate documents that could be modified for the project at hand. Although lawyers in large firms today probably work just as hard as those over fifty years ago did, the culture is very different. At the time, it was acceptable for junior lawyers to be treated rudely and at times worse. It was not uncommon for certain senior partners, when dissatisfied with a lawyer's work product, to actually throw the document at the lawyer to show their contempt.

The firm had a partner, Arnold Goldberg, whose major responsibility was not law practice but the assignment of associates to partners. Two vignettes remain in my memory. Several weeks into my employment, my girlfriend at the time was attacked in her home vestibule. She was not seriously hurt, but she remained in the hospital for a few days. I took a day off to visit her and supply her with necessities. The next day, I returned to the office and got a call from Goldberg, who asked about my absence. I explained the circumstance and he said, "Is it over?" In my naiveté, my first reaction was that he was expressing concern for my lady friend. However, it soon became clear to me that he was implicitly delivering the message that I was not expected to be absent from the office again.

The second incident that stands out occurred a couple of months later. I was scheduled to meet for lunch a college friend from out of town whom I had not seen in several years. There were no cellphones at the time. We agreed to meet on a street corner in midtown at 12:30 p.m. About noon, Arnold stopped by my office and said a certain partner was meeting a client for lunch. He asked if I would accompany the partner and bring along a notepad. I explained that I was about to meet someone for lunch and had no way of getting in touch with him. Arnold said, "No problem. We will send a messenger to meet him at the corner and tell him you cannot make it."

A law-firm associate's experience in the early years can be very mixed. Occasionally, the new lawyer will accompany a senior partner to a trial or argument of an appeal and gain valuable experience. At other times, the associate's assignments can be menial—or worse. During my first years as an associate, the Department of Justice was conducting a criminal antitrust investigation of the building-maintenance industry in New York. Until World War II, most major office building owners conducted cleaning services by the owner's own staff. Some of the "extra" work that a commercial tenant might require, such as window cleaning and internal office cleaning, would be contracted out to small cleaning companies whose principals were mostly recent Jewish immigrants from Eastern Europe. After the war, the newer generation of developers began to contract out all of their building cleaning services, and many of the small mom-and-pop companies accordingly morphed into large businesses, many going public.

As the maintenance companies grew in size, certain of the "old country" practices remained in the shadows. When the small companies had competed for the tenants' "extra" cleaning work, there was an understanding that nobody should "take the bread out of the mouth" of another company when they "stole" the cleaning work. Accordingly, the company that gained the client account would pay a "reparation" to the losing company. Informal records were supposedly kept of these transactions to record who owed whom for what and how much.

The U.S. Department of Justice, having gotten wind of these practices, deemed them to be potential antitrust violations in restraint of trade. The government served document subpoenas on all of the major building-maintenance companies in New York City, seeking to find evidence of these practices.

In the early 1970s, electronic document storage had not yet emerged in the business world. In commercial litigations in the courts, lawyers followed the long-standing practice of requesting documents from the adverse party to attempt to prove their case. Parties responding to these requests would often make available the requested documents by inviting the requesting lawyers to visit company warehouses where the documents were stored. Very often, given the very broad requests that lawyers typically make, there could be millions of documents responsive to the requests stored in these warehouses. I recall boarding airplanes during brutal winters for places in the Midwest I had never heard of and then taking a taxi to a huge warehouse where I would be greeted and led to the storage rooms. It seemed that every time I would do this, it would just happen that the heat was turned off so that I had to rummage through boxes wearing multiple layers of clothing. Of course, unless one found a needle-in-the-haystack "smoking gun," these excursions were mostly worthless.

In the building-maintenance investigation, the government served its typical sweeping subpoenas on each of the targeted companies. It was my job as the low man on the totem pole to spend weeks reviewing our client's responsive documents that would then be copied and turned over to the grand jury empaneled by the government. Talk about absurdity. Among the responsive documents were several hundred thousand daily logs of bathroom cleaners employed by the company in buildings they serviced. I suggested to the partner in charge of my work that it might be a waste of time for me to review these documents, because I thought it highly unlikely that these forms, with checked boxes to confirm that matters such as toilet paper and sanitary napkin replacements had been carried out in each bathroom, would likely yield evidence of an antitrust conspiracy. However, faithful to our commitment not to be caught by surprise, I was told to review "every document." So I spent the week reviewing thousands of the bathroom cleaners' forms wondering if one of them just might have a notation along the lines of, "We owe *X* maintenance company *Y* dollars for taking its tenant work at 100 Broadway." Fat chance. As it turned out, the evidence the government was looking for was all in small notebooks that were kept by the heads of the companies in their private quarters. Locating, copying, reviewing, and producing billions of documents were arguably worthless tasks. I really had not anticipated in law school that I would be awarded this prestigious assignment.

Although I did not expect to spend my career at Kaye Scholer or any large law firm, I certainly learned a lot in my years there. One of the most satisfying experiences was the opportunity to work with the recently retired Chief Judge of the New York Court of Appeals, Stanley H. Fuld. At the end of 1973, upon reaching age seventy, he was mandatorily retired from the Court, having spent many years there, first as an interim appointee of former Governor Thomas Dewey, the unsuccessful Republican candidate for President in 1948, and then by election.

Fuld had been an intellectual star as a young assistant when Dewey was the District Attorney in Manhattan. During his decades of service on New York's highest court, Fuld was regarded, together with Chief Judge Traynor of the California Supreme Court, as one of the most thoughtful, erudite jurists in the country. In January 1974, Fuld came to Kaye Scholer "of counsel" and brought with him his last law clerk, Sidney H. Stein (now a senior U.S. District Judge), with whom I started a law firm years later. Along with Stein, I was assigned to work with Fuld.

One of the cases the New York Court of Appeals had decided in 1949 was the so-called Stuyvesant Town case. That large housing development had been constructed in Manhattan by the Metropolitan Life Insurance Company after World War II. The operative agreement for tenants had a "whites only" clause, preventing any non-whites from leasing apartments. A legal challenge to this provision reached the New York Court of Appeals, and little remembered today, the Court voted 4–3 to uphold the legitimacy of the racial exclusion. Ahead of his time, Fuld penned a beautiful dissent, finding that enforcement of the clause constituted unconstitutional racial discrimination. Fortunately, superseding legislation in New York later outlawed the discriminatory practice.

In the mid-1990s, when I was Chairman of the Commercial and Federal Litigation Section of the New York State Bar

Association, I urged our Section to create an award in Judge Fuld's name, recognizing his contributions to scholarship. He was the first recipient of the award, and I asked Chief Judge Judith S. Kaye to present it at the annual meeting of the Association. Before the event, I visited Judge Fuld, then ninety-three years of age, and asked him what case stood out in his mind in his decades of service on the Court. He reflected for a moment and said, "My dissent in the Stuyvesant Town case." I wrote an article about the Stuyvesant Town case and Judge Fuld's dissent in the *New York Bar Journal* in 2015.

There is a true story that I have told about Judge Fuld. I went to work for him immediately upon his arrival at Kaye Scholer and was sent off to the library to do several days of legal research for a client. This was in the era before desktop computers, computerized legal research, and the internet. On my third day, Judge Fuld's assistant called the law-firm librarian to say that Judge Fuld would like to see me in his office. Before visiting Judge Fuld, I laid out before me in my little cubicle several law books with the key cases, trying to commit them to memory. I then walked into his office, and he asked me to sit down. Fuld looked at me and said, "Mark, I want to ask you something." I braced myself for what I expected would be a penetrating question from this great jurist. He then said, "Mark, how do I fill out these damn timesheets?" Of course, he was referring to these daily logs that lawyers in private practice are required to fill out to record time spent and billed to the client. Having worked for the government in the District Attorney's office and then on the Court since leaving law school in the 1920s, Fuld had never been required to do that.

Because I was fortunate to have had some basic trial training at NITA, the firm gave me a degree of responsibility that was not accorded most lawyers at my stage of practice. In the late 1970s, the American Bank and Trust Company failed and went into receivership and was taken over by the Federal Deposit Insurance Corporation. The FDIC retained Kaye Scholer to handle the many ongoing litigations in New York courts both for and against the bank. I was handed an ongoing case the bank had been pursuing against a man named John Samuels, an extremely wealthy individual of mysterious background, who had in recent years made his way into the New York social scene and was Chairman of the New York City Opera, New York City Ballet, and Vivian Beaumont Theater at Lincoln Center. He had taken a significant loan from the bank, which was in default, and claimed that a bank officer had relieved him of his obligation. (This contention was legally dubious, as under federal law, these kinds of defenses are generally not available against the FDIC as receiver.) Samuels was represented by the infamous lawyer Roy Cohn (a favorite of Donald J. Trump), who was known to try almost any tactic to win a case. When the trial approached, Cohn dropped out and allowed the case to be tried by one of his partners.

This trial was, for me, an experience in hell, but I learned a lot. The judge, Arnold Guy Fraiman, was a smart Ivy League–educated jurist who was a former Chief of the New York City Department of Investigations. He was reputed to have a terrible temperament. And his reputation was well earned. Fraiman could get angry at the slightest inconvenience or foot fault by a lawyer. In one well-known incident, Fraiman was on the bench awaiting the arrival of a prisoner being brought to court in a Department of Corrections bus. When the prisoner failed to appear in the courtroom at the required moment, Fraiman left the courtroom, went down the elevator and out to the street, and screamed at the bus driver for being late. In my first trial as lead attorney, I thought I would be in for a hard time—and I was. At one point, the judge asked me to approach and hand up a document. As I complied with his directive, he screamed at me, "Do not touch my bench." Although I was quite prepared on the law and the evidence, I could not have been adequately prepared for the judge's impatience at every turn. However, in this trial by fire, I prevailed.

In December 1975, a Midwestern wholesaler of magazines brought a lawsuit in federal court in Topeka, Kansas, against a competing wholesaler, ARA Services, and the eleven national distributors of consumer magazines. These distributors, in turn, obtained the magazines from the publishers. The plaintiff in the case, a family-run wholesaler business known as Palmer News, distributed magazines to hundreds of retailers in several Midwestern states, including Kansas, Oklahoma, and Nebraska. Palmer claimed that its competitor ARA Services had conspired with the eleven national distributors to afford ARA Services better pricing from the publishers than Palmer was accorded. It was a classic antitrust case.

The U.S. District Judge in Topeka, Richard Rogers, enjoyed the case, particularly because he liked meeting with the lawyers from New York City who would come out to Topeka to argue motions or attend conferences. He liked the experience so much that on a number of occasions, to make it more convenient for the New York lawyers, he traveled from the main courthouse in Topeka to a small courthouse in Kansas City, Kansas, a stepchild of Kansas City, Missouri, that sat across the Missouri River.

My law firm, Kaye Scholer, together with the law firm of Weil, Gotshal & Manges, acted as colead counsel for the eleven national distributor defendants, each of which had its own individual lawyers as well. One of these lawyers was John L. Eastman, the brother of Linda McCartney, Beatle Paul McCartney's sister. He was happy to leave much of the strategy to other lawyers, as he focused most of his attention on his legal work for The Beatles. My job as an associate was to partner with two associates at Weil to handle many of the depositions that took place throughout the Midwest. Some of these individual depositions lasted as long as three weeks—something that would never happen today, as the rules in the federal courts now generally limit depositions to a day each.

One by one, a number of the individual national distributor defendants settled with the plaintiff. The lead lawyers for the plaintiff and I put together a stipulation to end the case against the Kaye Scholer client and we contacted the judge's chambers to seek his approval. To our surprise, the judge got on the phone and told us that he wanted us to come out personally, so that he and his clerk could take us to lunch. Sure enough, we flew to Topeka, met Judge Rogers in his chambers, and he immediately approved the settlement. We then piled into his law clerk's car and traveled a few blocks to a bank building with a lunch club on the top floor.

From my travels to many small cities like Topeka, I had learned that lunch clubs on the tops of banks were typically the place where lawyers, judges, and politicians met. Upon reaching the top floor and entering the club, Judge Rogers—who had been very popular as a leader in the Kansas Legislature before his appointment to the bench—took me by the hand and walked me over to an older man who was talking to several people. He greeted the judge warmly. Judge Rogers shook his hand and said, "I'd like you to meet my good friend Mark, a great lawyer from New York." The older man shook my hand and said, "Really great to meet you." The older man was Alf Landon, then in his nineties, who had been the unsuccessful Republican candidate for President in 1936 against Franklin D. Roosevelt. He was also the father of the future senator from Kansas, Nancy Landon Kassebaum.

CHAPTER 13

A MIDTOWN SUICIDE

The year 1975 was a bleak one in New York City. The "Big Apple" was on the verge of defaulting on its bonds, which led to New York State intervention. At the time, President Gerald Ford initially declined to provide federal aid to the city – a decision reflected in a sarcastic headline in the *New York Daily News* that read, "FORD TO CITY: DROP DEAD." The city government was forced to lay off thousands of employees, defer wage increases, and severely cut back public services, even as crime rates rose sharply. Equally grim, just outside the city, 1975 saw the trial of Ronald DeFeo Jr., who was accused of murdering his parents and four siblings in Amityville, Long Island—the case on which the book and film *The Amityville Horror* were based. To cap off the year, in December, a bomb exploded at LaGuardia Airport, killing and injuring many people.

At the heart of New York City, behind Grand Central Terminal, the famous Pan Am skyscraper—built over a decade earlier with its celebrated heliport on the roof—dominated midtown. On February 4, 1975, Eli Black of United Brands

Company entered his office on the forty-fourth floor of the building. He was then the Chairman of this major conglomerate, which included the United Fruit Company, which produces Chiquita bananas. Black approached the plate-glass window of his office, shattered it with his briefcase, and jumped out, his body splattering on the street below.

Two months later, United Brands revealed publicly that Black had made a secret agreement with the President of Honduras, paying him $1.25 million from a bank account in Europe with the promise of a second payment in that amount, in return for that country's lowering the export tax on the company's bananas. In short order, the House and Senate convened congressional investigations; the Securities and Exchange Commission launched its own investigation; and private plaintiffs' lawyers commenced a series of class actions and so-called derivative actions, claiming that United Brands had failed to disclose that it was bribing foreign officials. The United Brands Board of Directors called upon the law firm with which I was associated, Kaye Scholer, to coordinate and oversee the defense of all of these actions and proceedings. This included a sweeping review of the company's activities abroad to determine whether there were other instances of bribery of foreign officials. As a fairly junior associate, I was assigned to assist in handling these litigations, putting my legal education in overdrive. One of my early assignments was, together with another associate, to search Eli's Black's desk and offices. These searches revealed some very sad communications between Black and others, which suggested events that likely led up to the suicide.

These events coincided with a number of evolving trends in law practice. One of these was the emergence of boutique "white-collar" law firms, populated largely by former federal prosecutors, to assist the major Wall Street law firms in corporate investigations and to represent corporate officials, who would need individual legal representation separate from their corporate employers.

During the course of the investigation initiated by the SEC, I represented United Brands in a deposition of Price Waterhouse & Co., the Company's accountants. The SEC was seeking to determine what, if anything, United Brands' accountants knew about foreign payments. At one of the depositions, I recall the senior partner from the Cravath firm, representing these accountants, was accompanied by a fairly young lawyer named Deborah Batts. She later was appointed by the President as a U.S. District Judge for the Southern District of New York.

One of the more interesting aspects of the SEC's investigation was a new legal theory being advanced by the then Director of Enforcement, Stanley Sporkin (who later became the General Counsel of the Central Intelligence Agency and then a U.S. District Judge). Traditionally, claims alleging failures to disclose material information to investors involved a company's misrepresenting its financial health, or omitting relevant information when disclosures were made. Sporkin advanced the theory that in the case of United Brands (and other companies under investigation), the failure to disclose the fact that a company's ongoing, significant business relations depended on bribery was itself an actionable nondisclosure, notwithstanding the fact that the amounts involved in the bribery itself might be relatively insignificant. With the ultimate settlements, the legal issue was never resolved in the United Brands cases, but today, a company's failure to disclose significant illegal conduct may well give rise to securities fraud liability if other pleading requirements are satisfied. Moreover, as a result of the United Brands scandal and several other similar cases, Congress enacted the Foreign Corrupt Practices Act of 1976, which makes it a serious federal crime for an individual or company subject to U.S. jurisdiction to pay bribes or gratuities to a foreign official.

This entire experience gave me an invaluable education on the nuts and bolts of high-stakes corporate litigation, behind-the-scenes lawyering strategy, and settlement techniques. The lessons would serve me well in the years to come.

CHAPTER 14

STRIKING OUT ON MY OWN

At some point, I began to feel wanderlust and started thinking about the next chapter in my career. Several well-regarded lawyers of my vintage had left two large New York City law firms to form the first of what became known as litigation "boutiques." The environment was right for this. Some of the institutional bonds between business clients and their white-shoe law firms were loosening. At the same time, clients began to consider giving work to smaller firms that they felt would give them better attention and serve them more efficiently. Also, more so than today, major law firms were willing to subcontract out legal work to these "spin-off" law firms, which would remain loyal to the mother ship and not try to compete for clients. An early example of this was the Olwine Connelly law firm, which spun off from the Cravath law firm in the 1950s largely to help service Cravath's important client, IBM.

My former colleague at Kaye Scholer, Sidney Stein, a talented lawyer who had been Judge Fuld's last clerk, had some years before left Kaye Scholer for another firm, Paul Weiss. He and I began to have occasional lunches and drinks to discuss the possibility of starting a boutique law firm to concentrate on litigation. I knew almost nothing about the business of law, except that I was convinced that the success of any startup venture required us to take into account several realities: First, that our initial source of clients would be obtained by the grace of our current law firms, who could refer clients to us or retain us as cocounsel in instances in which they needed our assistance. Second, we would concentrate on litigation and not try to be all things to all people. This, in turn, provided two advantages: one, that as a firm we could handle matters of a depth and complexity that a single litigator could not; and two, that by concentrating only in litigation, we would be less of a threat to lawyers who referred us matters, knowing that we were not in a position to steal their clients by offering a broad range of services.

Stein and I spent the better part of a year meeting with colleagues at other law firms who might be interested in forming a firm. Several expressed initial interest but then backed away. At the time, I was reminded of the 1952 movie *High Noon*, in which Gary Cooper tried to enlist a group of volunteers to meet the train arriving at the western town at noon. The train was expected to have aboard a gang of outlaws who would be returning to the town to obtain vengeance after their release from prison. Gary Cooper played the town sheriff. One of the deputies he tried to recruit to assist him in the anticipated gun fight was played by actor Lloyd Bridges. He agreed to sign up but then learned that he and Cooper were the only ones who would meet the outlaws, at which point he backed off, apologizing that he had a wife and children and didn't want to take the risk. As we tried to put together a new firm, a number of my lawyer colleagues demurred and reminded me of Lloyd Bridges.

By the fall of 1981, Stein and I had put together a group of five lawyers who were prepared to take the plunge. I recruited Ed Friedman, an associate at Kaye Scholer several years younger than me. Stein introduced me to David Ellenhorn, an experienced trial lawyer who had been a partner at several major firms and who most recently had served as Chief Counsel to New York's Special Investigations Commission. Stein also introduced me to Bruce Kaplan, another Paul Weiss alumnus, who most recently served as Chief Assistant Corporation Counsel for the City of New York. All four of them were Harvard or Yale graduates, or both. Stein, Zauderer, Ellenhorn, Friedman & Kaplan was born. That firm (later renamed Stein, Zauderer, Ellenhorn, Frischer & Sharp and finally Solomon, Zauderer, Ellenhorn, Frischer & Sharp) lasted for decades. We were old-fashioned and were like a shoemaker's children without shoes: We never had a partnership agreement, although we always cautioned our clients never to follow that practice. We had no executive committee or chairman. And each year, we divided up our profits on a napkin after some shuttle diplomacy by a partner who would write down the proposed profit allocations and forge an agreement. But fortunately the bounty was always plentiful, so nobody walked away hurting.

CHAPTER 15

A LEAP OF FAITH

To plan our law-firm venture, each of us had an assignment. Mine was to find a source of funding, as not all of us were prepared to invest whatever money we had saved over the years. I was told there was a group of young women who worked in the private bank of Manufacturers Hanover Trust Company, which had previously funded a group of lawyers that we knew. I made an appointment and showed up at the bank. There were the three smartly attired blonde women: One was Muffy, another was Buffy, and the third may have been Tuffy. I imagined they had all attended exclusive prep schools, probably in Connecticut. I was shown through a door into a back room out of sight of the teller windows. I had never been any place at a bank beyond the teller windows. I sat down in a comfortable, softly padded wing chair. An older man in a serving jacket, wearing white gloves, poured me a cup of coffee from a silver pitcher.

The lead banker welcomed me and asked how they could help. I said we were starting a law firm and were seeking a line of credit. "No problem; how much would you like?" I looked her in the eye and uttered a dollar number that seemed ridiculously high, but she didn't flinch. "No problem," she said again. "We will just need a budget." I asked her exactly what she meant, and she said, "You know—just estimated income and expenses for the first year." Somewhat naively, I told her that I really did not know what clients we would have the first year. She told me to just do the best I could.

I settled in to figure out how to execute this task. On the expense side, I put together a rough estimate of projected monthly expenses for the first year. But, how to estimate income? Then I had an idea. I knew there were five of us. I figured we would bill our time at the rate our current firms had then been charging—$130 per hour. I also assumed we would bill and collect for an average of 1,600 hours each per year. I then did the multiplication: 130 x 5 x 1600. I looked at the number, compared it to the estimated expenses, and what do you know? We had just turned a profit! I sent this to the bank and in short order we had our line of credit.

The next thing we had to resolve was how to utilize this line of credit to maintain ourselves. All of my partners were married with children; I was the only single partner. We determined who needed the most weekly income and used that amount to fix a biweekly draw for all of us on the line of credit. That way, nobody had to use his savings.

But we also had to make some decisions about how to spend our borrowed money, fully aware that we would be depleting our line of credit and going further into debt. One good decision we made was not to economize on our rental space, deciding we did not want to be perceived as a low-budget operation. So, we sublet first-class space from a major law firm. Instead of making a capital investment in furnishings, we rented attractive furniture from an office furniture rental company. Computer word processing was still relatively young. Knowing that producing paper product was a lawyer's stock in trade, we leased what was then state-of-the-art word processing equipment, at a time when universal desktop computers were several years away.

As I said farewell to my colleagues at Kaye Scholer, Professor Milton Handler, regarded by many as the dean of antitrust law, graciously wished me good luck. He said, "Although you won't have the financial success you would at a large, prestigious firm, you will have a very enjoyable practice." Some years later I recalled this parting observation and smiled, knowing that I had proved Professor Handler half wrong.

* * * * *

I remember vividly that mixed feeling of excitement and fear on October 1, 1981, when I left my big firm and my paycheck stopped. From that point on, it was sink or swim. There is no better motivator than fear. After two weeks, we took our first drawdown on our line of credit. Fortunately, circumstances coalesced that foretold a bright future. Through the courtesy of our prior law firms, we continued to work essentially as subcontractors on cases we had been handling at those firms. And as we had hoped, our former firms reached out to us for assistance in some major trials and fast-moving tender offer cases. After the first two weeks, we never had to draw again on our line of credit.

During the first year, our practices blossomed. And it was not just litigation. In one case, we represented an airline broker who claimed a substantial commission on the sale of several airplanes. We received a contingency fee for simply negotiating a settlement with a few phone calls. In another matter, we represented a major company bidding on the sale of new New York City subway cars to the Metropolitan Transportation Authority (MTA), for which we were paid at premium time rates plus a success fee based on each subway car for which a contract was awarded to our client. The client was awarded a contract for quite a few subway cars.

I soon realized that while hoping for lightning to strike, I had to have a plan for future professional development. I started by reinvigorating my professional relationships with lawyers I knew from my prior work, including senior partners at major law firms, often meeting lawyers for lunch or breakfast. The efforts brought rewards in the form of interesting and important work. Then, as often happens, chance brings about opportunity—or, perhaps as the saying goes, you have to work hard to make luck happen.

Beginning in the late 1970s, Circuit City Stores, which had begun as a small consumer electronics company in Richmond, Virginia, expanded rapidly throughout the country, eventually becoming a public company listed on the New York Stock Exchange. In 1981, Circuit City acquired the remnants of the bankrupt Lafayette Radio Electronics Company, a national company that cratered largely as a result of the decline in popularity of CB radio. Among the jewels in Lafayette's inventory were eight long-term, low-cost leases in the New York City metropolitan area that were acquired by Circuit City. This put Circuit City on a collision course with landlords; with a growing national competitor, Crazy Eddie; and with a local retailer, The Wiz ("Nobody Beats the Wiz"). At the same time, Circuit City rapidly expanded nationwide, and a decade later it had more than one hundred shopping centers under development in the United States.

One day I got a telephone call from a real-estate consultant working with Circuit City who asked me if I would handle a litigation involving Circuit City at a former Lafayette location on Union Square in New York City. We handled the matter successfully. Several months later, just before the July 4 holiday weekend in 1983, I received a call from Alan Wurtzel, the Chairman of Circuit City. Wurtzel was a Yale-educated lawyer who, among his many skills, was able to manage the company's legal affairs without an internal legal department, except when he had to turn to a Richmond law firm for certain corporate matters. Wurtzel had heard about the results in the Union Square case and asked to meet me for lunch at the Yale Club on Thursday before the holiday weekend.

When Lafeyette Radio had been in bankruptcy from 1980 to 1981, it had been leasing a large warehouse on Long Island where it maintained its central offices while it wound down its operations. The owner of the warehouse, a feisty banker and real-estate entrepreneur named Jack Farber, had sued Lafayette in the Bankruptcy Court for damage to the building and for use and occupancy (another term for rent). By agreement in that court, the Lafeyette bankruptcy case was closed with the understanding that Farber's claims would continue against Circuit City in the New York State Court in Queens, New York. Farber was no shrinking violet. As Chairman of the Flushing National Bank a decade earlier, he had brought a successful lawsuit challenging New York City's suspension of interest payments on MAC bonds during New York City's financial crisis. Farber won his case in the New York Court of Appeals, which ruled the suspension of interest payments unconstitutional.

At my lunch with Wurtzel, one of the circumstances that became apparent was that one of Farber's lawyers was politically connected in the Queens trial court, which raised concern about the neutrality of the forum. Wurtzel said, "We have a local Long Island lawyer handling the matter, but please take over." We had to come up with a strategy. At the time, under the applicable federal statute, a defendant in Circuit City's position could remove the action to federal court, but only within thirty days of the creation of a "paper" that demonstrated so-called "diversity of citizenship," one of the grounds for federal court jurisdiction (in other words, the plaintiff and defendant must be citizens of different states).

Under applicable case law, Farber's deposition, which had just been taken days before, qualified as the requisite "paper." But we still had to demonstrate diversity of citizenship. In his original court complaint, Farber had alleged that he was a resident of New York, suggesting that New York State was his place of "citizenship." That would mean that since Lafeyette had been a New York corporation, there would be no grounds for diversity federal jurisdiction. However, at his recent deposition, Farber testified that he was residing in Florida. We suspected that he had permanently changed his residence to Florida for tax reasons, as many wealthy New Yorkers do. We immediately retained a private investigator in Florida who located Farber's home, took pictures of his car in the driveway, and obtained voting records in which Farber had declared Florida to be his permanent residence. The investigators provided us with copies of the declaration and pictures of Farber's car in his Florida driveway.

Over the July 4 weekend, we worked to prepare the necessary papers for removal to federal court. On Tuesday morning, we walked into the state court in Queens where the case was scheduled to go to trial and filed the removal petition. From that moment on, the state court had no jurisdiction over the case. With the matter now technically in federal court, the U.S. District Court for the Eastern District of New York on Long Island, we immediately served a flurry of deposition notices for further discovery. The case was assigned to newly appointed U.S. District Judge Leonard D. Wexler.

Farber's lawyers, taken by surprise, filed a motion in the federal court to remand the case to state court. Judge Wexler called a conference. He suggested that Farber's lawyer allow the case to remain in the federal court because he would conduct the trial soon. Farber's lawyers agreed. However, that did not happen for over two years. Eventually, the case was tried, Farber lost, and he took an appeal to the United States Court of Appeals for the Second Circuit. Most of Judge Wexler's decision was affirmed while a relatively small part of the case was remanded to him for a second trial. At the end, Farber was awarded pennies on the dollar.

That opportunity to represent Circuit City opened the floodgates. Over the next dozen years, I attended hearings and conducted trials in many states where Circuit City had interests, many of them involving real estate and, in one case, a battle ensued over television advertising between Circuit City and its rival in New York City, Crazy Eddie. Yet another case involved the patent on the ubiquitous flashing colon that appears as 12:00 a.m. on every clock on every electronic device and home appliance. Circuit City sold thousands of them.

CHAPTER 16

NO WATER

Water is a big deal in Texas. One day I was alerted to an emergency in San Antonio, where Circuit City had purchased a large tract of land to develop a shopping center. The adjoining landowner wanted to participate in the development but was rebuffed by Circuit City. It brought a lawsuit in Texas state court to enjoin the opening of the shopping center, where two hundred employees were about to start work, based on its claim that the paving of the new shopping center diverted water from the adjoining property in violation of Texas statutes. The local judge issued a temporary restraining order preventing the shopping center from opening. Circuit City asked me to get on a plane and get this problem solved as soon as possible.

All litigators know that if you appear in a far-away jurisdiction (and in New York City, sometimes in a different borough), you need to retain a well-known local lawyer as cocounsel. I searched my Rolodex but did not see the name of anybody I knew in San Antonio. The best I could do was to contact a lawyer from Fort Worth who came highly recommended, and we arranged to meet that night in San Antonio. Meanwhile, he contacted the adversary lawyer and the court to arrange for a continued hearing the next day on the temporary restraining order.

As I entered the Bexar County courthouse in San Antonio the following morning, almost all the lawyers were wearing cowboy boots (I felt out of place in my black wingtips) and I saw notices of ranch foreclosures tacked to the walls. We found the judge's courtroom, shook hands with the adversary lawyer, and waited for the judge to arrive. A few minutes later, the judge appeared, took his seat on the bench, and called the case. My cocounsel stood up, addressed the court, and said, "Your Honor, I would like to introduce and move for admission my cocounsel Mark Zauderer from New York City. He is representing Circuit City Stores together with me." The judge looked directly at me and snarled, "New York? I was there once. I really did not like the place."

Any lawyer in my situation would know that he or she was not in for a good day. I then stood up and responded, "Your Honor, it's a privilege and a pleasure for me to be in this courthouse again." The judge said, "Oh, you have been here before?" I responded, "Yes, your honor, this is the very courthouse where I finalized the adoption of my son, Daniel, six years ago." The judge exclaimed, "That's great! We love doing adoptions here in Texas! Welcome." I breathed a sigh of relief, knowing that I was unlikely ever to be able to pull a rabbit out of a hat that way again.

Meanwhile, back on the home front, things were heating up in New York City. Brush fires were breaking out in a number of places. After Circuit City had taken over the former Lafeyette Radio locations in New York City, Circuit City invested considerable sums in expanding in the New York City market, coming head-to-head with electronics retailer Crazy Eddie. Circuit City's advertising agency was running ten television advertisements, each of them spoofing the loud advertising spokesman for Crazy Eddie, the actor Jerry Carroll. One of these scenes depicted a supposed Crazy "Eddie" sitting in a confessional booth with a sign, "The Confessions of Crazy Eddie." The actor leaned over and whispered through the screen, supposedly to a priest, "I don't tell the customers that I really won't give them my lowest price unless they ask me for it." Crazy Eddie had received letters from outraged viewers who thought the advertisement was sacrilegious. This supposedly demonstrated confusion among the public, because viewers did not understand that the ad was generated by Circuit City—not Crazy Eddie.

Consumer confusion is the touchstone for asserting a claim in federal court under a statute known as the Lanham Act. Crazy Eddie filed a complaint in the U.S. District Court in Manhattan, asking the court for a temporary restraining order barring the ad from television, as well as the nine other advertisements that were running. After an evidentiary hearing, the judge, Mary Johnson Lowe, denied the injunction as to nine advertisements, while Circuit City voluntarily withdrew the one entitled "The Confessions of Crazy Eddie." The remaining nine advertisements significantly helped Circuit City expand in the New York market.

CHAPTER 17

SPREADING MY WINGS

Although I was making significant progress in expanding my practice, I was aware that one of the ways that prospective clients judge you is not just by your skills, which may be difficult for them to evaluate, but by the company you keep. In my years as an associate at a large firm, I had the good fortune to litigate with, and against, some of the best lawyers in New York. I was happy just to see them in action in the boardroom or the courtroom. I also thought about how I could continue to learn from them while enhancing my visibility in the legal community.

I began by cobbling together a course in commercial litigation for the Practising Law Institute, a leading not-for-profit institution well-known to lawyers. I called several prominent senior partners that I knew in major law firms to ask them to join me in a continuing legal education panel that I would chair. At the time, mandatory continuing legal education for lawyers was taking hold in many states, and organizations such as PLI were trying to meet the demand. I organized the panel, and we made a live presentation in both New York City and San Francisco (remote programs by Zoom were still decades away). I then created a similar course for the New York State Bar Association. At the time, it was routine for that Association to distribute printed brochures advertising a program which displayed an enlarged picture of the Chair along with the pictures of the other panel members. My picture as Chair appeared above the pictures of all the panel members, each of whom was far better known than me at the time.

Shortly afterwards, I was asked by a colleague, Bob Haig, to join the newly formed Commercial & Federal Litigation Section of the New York State Bar Association. After participating for several years in many projects involving New York State's court procedures, I was elected Chair of the Section. In 1992, I was appointed by New York's Chief Administrative Judge to the Advisory Committee on Civil Practice, where I have served for thirty-two years. This body is comprised of academics and experienced practitioners who draft proposed laws for the New York State Legislature that govern trial practice in the courts. This work has always helped me as a practicing lawyer to keep up with the relevant rules that govern our trial practice. I also joined the Federal Bar Council, the leading bar association of federal judges and practitioners in the federal courts within the Second Circuit. Years later, I was privileged to serve as President of that organization.

CHAPTER 18

WORKING FOR THE JUDGES AND THE COURT SYSTEM

Perhaps contrary to popular belief, the most successful lawyers are not obsessed with "making money." Most love their work and look forward to the opportunity to be relied upon for important matters, even if they are not compensated. It is simply a myth that all lawyers are interested only in money. Many lawyers I know have found the highest degree of satisfaction handling matters that pay nothing. That has been true for me in the course of my career.

In 1991, Mario Cuomo had been Governor of New York for eight years. The Chief Judge of the New York Court of Appeals at the time was a brilliant lawyer, Sol Wachtler, who had been appointed to that position by Cuomo. In New York, the Chief Judge has two separate constitutional responsibilities. He or she serves on New York's highest court, the Court of Appeals.

That is a judicial function. But the second position is that of the Chief Judge of the State of New York, responsible for overseeing the entire state court system. In that capacity, the Chief Judge is like a chief executive officer of a corporation. The court system's analog of a board of directors is the Administrative Board, which consists of the Chief Judge of the State and the Presiding Justice of each of the state's four Appellate Divisions (the court just below the Court of Appeals). With the approval of the Administrative Board, the Chief Judge appoints the equivalent of a chief operating officer, known as the Chief Administrator or Chief Administrative Judge, who oversees the administration of the courts consistent with the policies established by the Administrative Board. The New York court system is enormous and difficult to administer. The State has over three thousand judges in its sprawling sixty-two counties, with thousands of nonjudicial employees and contracts with many unions. Its annual budget today is well over $2 billion.

Governor Cuomo and Chief Judge Wachtler were two men who had respect for the courts but viewed them from two different perches. As a Democratic Governor, Mario Cuomo had appointed both Republicans and Democrats to the high court, as well as the Court's first female judge (later appointed Chief Judge), Judith S. Kaye. Some say that Cuomo appointed Wachtler as Chief Judge in part to sidetrack him from running against Cuomo as a Republican candidate for Governor.

In 1991, growing frustrated with the state budget's allocation for the massive court system, Chief Judge Wachtler, on behalf of the entire Judiciary, brought a lawsuit against Governor Cuomo and the New York State Legislature over what he contended was inadequate funding for the courts. The lawsuit, brought in state court in Albany, advanced two theories: The first, the narrow one, that the State Constitution required the Judiciary's budget, when presented to the Governor by the Chief Judge, to be passed on to the Legislature "without revision." Cuomo, to Wachtler's chagrin, had slashed the proposed budget before submitting it to the Legislature. Wachtler's second theory was that the Judiciary, as an independent branch of government, was entitled to a reasonable level of funding sufficient for it to perform its functions. That theory had been raised at the time in litigation in other states.

The Chief Judge was initially represented by counsel within the state's Office of Court Administration. Judge Wachtler and his Chief Administrator, Matthew T. Crosson, and Deputy Chief Administrator, Jonathan Lippman (later Chief Judge of the State), then reached out for volunteers among prominent lawyers to assist in the effort. I received a call and was happy to participate and brought with me three lawyers from my firm to assist me. The pace was frantic, as the trial judge in Albany, Lawrence Kahn, scheduled a trial only a few weeks away. Judge Kahn later became a federal judge and, as fellow Union College graduates, we eventually became good friends. (In 2011 Judge Kahn asked me to moderate a discussion on neuroscience and the law at the Second Circuit Judicial Conference.)

I camped out at an office provided to me at the Office of Court Administration on lower Broadway, as our team took, or defended, four simultaneous depositions each day. The Governor was not only pushing back on the legal theories of the case, but claiming the Judiciary was wasting much of its allocated funds. Of course, Wachtler disputed that. I was selected by Wachtler as the lead lawyer to try the case in Albany. Around the same time, Governor Cuomo retained my former law-school classmate, Kenneth Feinberg (who had built a prominent reputation as fund administrator in national compensation proceedings, which later included the September 11 Fund and many others). He commenced a lawsuit in federal court on behalf of Cuomo in an attempt to derail the state-court trial. The federal judge promptly dismissed that case.

Ten days before trial, I was in an Office of Court Administration conference room representing a Deputy Administrative Judge at his deposition when someone walked in to the deposition room and asked us to take a break. I stepped out of the room and was told that someone in the Legislature had just brokered a telephone call between Governor Cuomo and Judge Wachtler. They had agreed to settle their dispute. I went back into the room, announced that the deposition was ended, packed up my briefcase, and left the office for good. My job was over. Later, Judge Wachtler held a reception for those of us who had helped in the litigation. He also sent me two gracious personal letters, and Chief Administrator Crosson sent me a short note about an article in the *Law Journal* discussing the litigation, saying, "The only thing they missed in the article was that silver bullet you left here." The reference to the Lone Ranger was flattering. These letters remain on my office wall today.

CHAPTER 19

THE COMMISSION ON THE JURY

Chief Judge Judith S. Kaye was a commercial litigator before being chosen as an Associate Judge of the New York Court of Appeals and later Chief Judge. She always retained the perspective of a trial lawyer, and through that lens she oversaw the vast New York court system operating in sixty-two counties. In the 1990s, Judge Kaye appointed Paul Weiss partner Colleen McMahon (now a senior U.S. District Judge) to chair a commission to recommend changes to New York's antiquated laws governing jury service. Among the changes made were to eliminate disqualifications and exemptions that either forbade jury service by certain groups of people or provided grounds for excusal. For example, morticians and lawyers were no longer exempted from jury service, and the term of potential jury service for those who were not selected to serve on a jury was reduced.

In 2003, Judge Kaye decided to remedy a situation she found most troubling: More than sixty thousand New York citizens were called for potential jury service each year, but only about 20 percent of them actually served on a jury. Given the right of citizens to serve on juries as well as the obligation to do so, she wanted to know why this was the case. She asked me to chair a new Jury Commission. At first I was hesitant, because in my experience, reports prepared by blue-ribbon panels often are placed on a shelf to gather dust. But Judge Kaye assured me, "Mark, whatever your panel recommends, we will implement." I then assembled a distinguished group of judges and practicing lawyers from different segments of the legal community (it included Loretta Lynch, later Attorney General of the United States), as well as a nonlawyer citizen. We were determined to answer Judge Kaye's question. My Commission on the Jury held seven public hearings throughout New York State, heard 140 witnesses, and solicited written submissions from people who had views. And we heard some very strong views.

One of the unusual features of the New York State courts is that in civil cases, of which there are thousands each year, judges overseeing trials are not required to be physically present to oversee the *voir dire* process, during which lawyers question prospective jurors to determine bias or any other factors that suggest a person should not serve on a case. Unlike in the federal courts and most states, lawyers in New York have the right to question jurors themselves in civil cases rather than relying on the judge to do so. As most people are aware, citizens can be excused from service either for "cause" (because their bias or inability to serve is demonstrated) or by a lawyer's exercise of a peremptory challenge for any reason that is not an illegal reason, such as racial or ethnic discrimination. This right to exercise peremptory challenges is passionately protected by New York trial lawyers. Another feature peculiar to New York is that the law allows a relatively high number of peremptory challenges to eliminate jurors—as many as twenty in a serious felony case. As a result of the first Jury Commission project under Colleen McMahon, the permitted number of peremptory challenges in civil cases had been reduced to three challenges per side—something that had not been welcomed by trial lawyers.

At the start of our hearings, we heard testimony from those with strong feelings about these issues. Many of the trial judges, represented by their professional organization, the Association of Supreme Court Justices, were fearful that we would recommend legislation to require judges to attend the civil voir dire process, arguing that they simply did not have the time, given their other responsibilities. Trial lawyer groups voiced their concern that a further reduction of the number of permissible peremptory challenges would be recommended. Another group argued that peremptory objections should be eliminated entirely. Several other witnesses objected to the ongoing use by lawyers of so-called "consent excusals"—by agreement of counsel when there was neither grounds for cause excusal, or the use of a peremptory challenge—arguing that the practice violated a person's right to serve on a jury.

Finally, to get to the bottom of the question as to why such a small percentage of those called to jury service actually served, we came across two significant but difficult-to-quantify features of our system: Since judicial supervision was not required, in places such as New York City, a citizen would show up at the court in the morning, view a short film about the importance of jury service, and then be put in a windowless room where the jurors were questioned by the lawyers without a judge present. During the questioning, the lawyers might have a dispute concerning the propriety of certain questions or whether the juror should be excused for cause. They would then leave the room to find an on-duty judge or judicial hearing officer to resolve the dispute, leaving the citizens to just sit and wait. Most of them would end up being dismissed or excused for one reason or another, with their lack of enthusiasm and even frustration prompting many asserted excuses. They would go home having spent the day without even having seen someone in black robes.

To make matters worse, in our hearings we found that there was a sharp difference in practice between, on the one hand, the courts in New York City and its environs, and, on the other hand, courts upstate. In New York City, court officials would summon candidates for perhaps three anticipated trials at the same time, knowing that in all likelihood, two of the three cases would settle before trial, once the actual jurors were picked and could be evaluated by the lawyers. In upstate New York, as one of the administrative judges testified, this practice would be regarded as highly offensive and an abuse of citizens' time. This judge said that if he held a settlement conference the day before the jury was picked and the parties were far apart, and then the lawyers reached a settlement the next morning after the jury was picked, he would no longer consider those lawyers welcome in this court. He felt that would be a terrible abuse of citizens' time.

Because our twenty-eight-member Commission was comprised of people from different parts of the legal community, there were different views on all of these issues. I recognized that for us to do anything meaningful, we needed to find consensus on at least some important issues. With some subtle diplomacy behind the scenes, I was able to forge agreement on some major changes that would improve citizen participation in the jury process. These recommendations, many of which were implemented, included steps to reduce the amount of unnecessary waiting time that jurors and prospective jurors must spend at the courthouse; improve communications with jurors; involve judicial personnel in interaction with jurors; and provide better amenities to jurors to minimize inconvenience.

Although I was finished with the Jury Commission work, Chief Judge Kaye was not finished with me. In 2005, the American Bar Association was focusing attention on our jury system, and Judge Kaye was eager to show her support for the effort. She asked me to conduct a series of educational town-hall meetings in half a dozen courthouses throughout New York State, starting with the New York Court of Appeals in Albany. She arranged to have a camera crew trail me to record the events. The Office of Court Administration arranged to have local high-school students at each location brought to the courthouse to participate in these town-hall meetings.

On Law Day 2005, Judge Kaye held a news conference outside the New York Court of Appeals, attended by the press and a number of state officials, to announce that I would be leading a discussion on the floor of the Court of Appeals, where over one hundred high-school students would be brought in, with whom I would engage in a dialog about the jury system. Some of them had the benefit of a brief classroom introduction to the topic so that they could meaningfully participate in this exercise.

With the students filling up the Court of Appeals courtroom, I walked around with a microphone to engage them in dialogue about the jury system, posing various questions to elicit their thoughts. After twenty or thirty minutes, I showed a film clip of the 1957 movie *Twelve Angry Men*, starring Henry Fonda, Lee J. Cobb, E. G. Marshall, and Jack Warden. In the movie, at the end of the trial the jurors had been charged on the law by the judge and were sent to the jury room to begin deliberations. As the jurors assembled in the room, the newly chosen foreman asked the others, "What do we do now?" I stopped the clip and then asked the students, "What should they do now?" Many hands shot up, and the answers they gave were impressive and inspired. Although none of them had yet reached the age of eighteen—the minimum age for voting or jury service—I was confident that the next generation of citizen jurors would serve us well.

Going around the State of New York proselytizing about the importance of jury service had its interesting moments unrelated to law. I experienced one of these on Law Day in 2004. The District Attorney in Warren County, Kate Hogan, a member of my Jury Commission, asked me to deliver remarks at an annual Law Day breakfast in Glens Falls. The citizens of that community take the celebration of this day very seriously. I explained to Kate that I had to be at the courthouse in Syracuse, New York, to conduct a town-hall meeting with members of the Judiciary and students later that morning, and it would be impossible for me to be in two places at virtually the same time. She said, "No problem. I'll get you there." Sure enough, as I finished my breakfast remarks in Glens Falls, an unmarked state police car waited for me at the back door of the breakfast hall and drove me at a speed close to one hundred miles per hour from there to Syracuse, depositing me at just the appointed hour at the courthouse. The drive was awe-inspiring, but quite unnerving, as I watched the countryside along the New York State Thruway fly past me. I thought to myself that my young son would enjoy this much more than I did.

CHAPTER 20
THE DIFFERENT DRUMMER

In the winter of 1983, I returned to New York from a ski trip to find the city a somewhat depressing place. The weather was cold and damp with the winter chill unbroken by sunlight. It was a weekend, and I saw an ad for the New York Boat Show. I had never been to a boat show; nor did I have any experience with boats other than as a passenger on scuba diving trips in the Caribbean. Entering the show and walking through the aisles at random, I stopped at a display presented by a boat dealer based on City Island, a historic area of fishermen and boat captains in the Bronx in New York City. On display was a twenty-six foot "cabin cruiser" that had basic accommodations for eating and sleeping on an overnight trip. I talked to the salesman, and something sparked an interest.

A week later, I visited the boatyard on City Island and met the salesman I had seen at the boat show. Before long I ordered the exact same boat model I had seen at the boat show, to be delivered in the spring. I rented a boat slip at the dealer's marina and took some basic instruction in boat handling. By the end of the summer, I was so taken by the experience that I traded the boat in for a larger boat, a thirty-three-foot version. (In comparing boats of different lengths, one has to keep in mind that the size of a boat is cubic, so that a thirty-three-foot boat might have twice the volume and weight of a twenty-six-foot boat.) Over the next two summers, I began to expand my cruises from City Island to the eastern end of Long Island Sound and then beyond to Block Island, Rhode Island—about 120 nautical miles from City Island at the western end. By the end of the second season, I was ready to move up to my next boat, a forty-two-foot motor yacht that, like my other two boats, I named *Different Drummer*.

The concept of "marching to the beat of a different drum" is certainly not one I conceived of. But, as both my personal and professional life became more and more involved with my desire to be at sea, I spent less and less time with friends and family on land. I felt that I had become a "different drummer." Even during winter months when my boat was hauled onto land, I would occasionally sit in a cabin aboard just to allow myself to think about the season past or the one to come.

In the 1980s, there was a trend on the East Coast for developers to purchase old family-run boat yards and convert them to cooperative or condominium boat slips, to be marketed to an expanding group of recreational boaters. I purchased a large boat slip in the newly developed South Minneford Yacht Club on the east side of City Island. The slip was the farthest from the shore and had a beautiful view looking across the Sound toward the Gold Coast of Long Island—*Great Gatsby* country. It was the perfect home for the new *Different Drummer*. While retaining ownership of the slip, I rented another slip at the Mamaroneck Beach & Yacht Club about six nautical miles away on the Sound and also established an offshore mooring near Hen Island, so I could sleep on the water securely moored, not depending on my anchor.

I later purchased a second boat that I named *Little Drummer*, which I berthed alongside *Different Drummer*. On some beautiful weekends, I would spend days and nights on the water on *Different Drummer*, shuttling into the Club on *Little Drummer*. Over time, *Different Drummer* became my office at sea, where I could isolate myself and read for days on end preparing for trials or appeals.

I realized that to take full advantage of my time at sea, I needed to have a full-time captain. My good luck brought me to meet Albert ("Bert") Daniels, an older man who was born and lived his entire life in Mamaroneck, New York. He was a Hollywood central casting example of an old salt and sea captain. Born in 1936, he had worked in a local boatyard where his father was the yard manager, and by age twelve he was ferrying people to nearby Hen Island. As a young adult, he served in the army and then the Coast Guard Reserve, operating marine craft of all kinds and teaching boating skills both to military personnel and civilians. While maintaining employment as a teacher for many years at a local school, he moonlighted in his own business, listening on a marine radio day and night for calls for help from boaters in distress. He would run out to Long Island Sound at any hour on his small boat to assist or tow the person in trouble.

Bert had retired some years before from his teaching job. He became the dockmaster at Minneford Yacht Club on City Island, where I owned my co-op boat slip. When I decided I needed a captain, Bert was ready to make this his last assignment. Although I was perfectly capable of running the yacht by myself, having an experienced hand on board created a new freedom and expanded my horizons in several ways.

Those not familiar with boating may not realize that a motor yacht of even modest size is a complex piece of machinery with many systems, both mechanical and electrical. It sits in a hostile salt-water environment, where its many components are under attack. Machinery breaks, pumps can fail, hoses get clogged, mechanical joints come loose, and just about anything destructive that can happen…will. A boat also has the mechanical features of a house, including toilets and sinks, a kitchen, and all of the utilities that one finds in a home kitchen, such as a refrigerator, a microwave, and even a dishwasher and laundry. Something will always need attention at any moment. Having an experienced hand on board to lend assistance before you reach a boatyard is more than helpful.

Navigating with a captain also makes life easier and much safer. Although Bert and I were both experienced with nautical charts and learned navigation skills before the proliferation of modern electronics, bad weather, fog, and difficult seas can make safe navigation a challenge. Having two people aboard is a big help. There were so many things that came naturally to Bert. Little by little, I was fortunate to learn many of his tricks of the trade, although I could never match his lifetime of experience.

In 2004, I was considering buying a new boat; however, I had another idea. I loved *Different Drummer*, but it was getting older, and had limitations on speed, and as a gas-powered, twin-engine boat, it had inherent safety compromises which diesel-powered boats did not. Its original twin 340-horsepower engines propelled the boat at only ten knots cruising at 3,000 RPMs—poor performance for a planing-hull boat. I contracted for a project at my regular boatyard in Old Saybrook, Connecticut, to completely gut *Different Drummer* and rebuild her as a diesel-powered boat. I would also convert her from mechanical operation (in such a traditional boat, wires connect the controls from the bridge to the engine room) to a fly-by-wire system with new, large diesel engines. The project involved four full-time people undertaking the conversion all winter as well as subcontractors fabricating parts. Holes were drilled in the bottom of the boat to accommodate the powerful exhaust of the new diesel engines: twin Cummins turbocharged diesel engines of 480 horsepower each. Two cranes opened the salon floor and lifted all of the machinery and wiring out of the engine room. New fuel tanks and exhaust systems were custom fabricated to fit the boat, new shafts were fitted, computers with backup were installed, and miles of wiring were replaced and routed. On the bridge, all of the old instruments were removed, a new panel was custom-designed, and the new instruments—both analog and digital—were custom-fitted. The electronics were also updated with a new radar system, multiple chart displays, GPS instruments, and an AIS receiver, among other things. (AIS is the system that commercial ships and aircraft have that allow them to know the identity, speed, and direction of other ships in the area.) To top it off, a new diesel generator was installed to power all facilities on board, including the three separate air-conditioning zones. I could remain at sea for days with all the conveniences of home and the office.

The memory of one summer day in the first season after the refit is etched in my mind. I had to appear in court briefly in downtown Manhattan. I called Captain Bert and asked him to have the boat ready at my slip in Mamaroneck. When the court conference ended about 9:45 a.m., I jumped on the subway and headed for Grand Central, switched to the Metro-North train, disembarked at the Mamaroneck station where my car was parked, and drove down to the Mamaroneck Beach & Yacht Club, where Bert had the engines running and the heavy shore electrical power cords disconnected and on board. As I boarded the boat, we immediately left the marina and the harbor at 12:30 p.m. I went below, took a quick shower in one of the comfortable staterooms, and changed into shorts and a polo shirt. *Different Drummer* was running down the Sound at her new cruising speed of 24.5 knots. We raced east for over a hundred miles on Long Island Sound until we reached the open waters of Rhode Island Sound. Then, as if rising out of the ocean, Block Island appeared. By 5:00 p.m., we were moored inside the protection of New Harbor on Block Island. It was time to make a gin and tonic, put my feet up, and reflect on one beautiful day.

Long Island Sound is one of the premier locations in the United States for recreational boaters. Created by the receding glacier some ten thousand years ago, the underwater bottom is strewn with terminal moraine, essentially rocks and boulders left behind. It has appealing bays and rivers easily accessed from the Sound, providing a great variety of boating experiences near quaint villages on both the northern Connecticut side and the southern New York side. But the Sound is full of hazards that provide economic sustenance to the boat-repair yards along the way.

One of the skills that boaters had to master was navigating safely to an intended destination both in good weather and bad (sometimes with no visibility), and during both day and night. Modern electronic instruments have made navigation easier and are probably responsible for attracting new boaters who have neither the time nor interest to learn traditional skills. But danger always lurks, particularly if one lacks knowledge beyond the ability to input data on a navigation computer. To understand this, one needs to be aware of some basic realities that have not changed with technological progress.

Mariners discovered a long time ago that magnetic north—the point toward which the compass needle is attracted—is not precisely the same as true north, that is, the theoretical point from which all lines of longitude descend, the point upon which the earth rotates. In fact, the point of magnetic north actually moves over time, so that the distance between magnetic north and true north changes. Which takes us to the classic nautical chart.

The nautical chart is, in and of itself, a magnificent instrument, developed and improved over time as more precise information on the position of land masses, and the depth of the oceans and smaller bodies of water, has been collected and documented. Before the advent of modern electronics, an international mariner who wanted to travel, say, from New York to England, could not plot a course relying on a single chart. Two realities come into play: First, a mariner usually wants to plot the shortest route from point A to point B. That course is always what is known as a "great circle route," which is along the edge of a plane that touches point A, point B, and the center of the earth. Second, a nautical chart is always a two-dimensional projection of the earth, which is actually a three-dimensional sphere.

Suppose you wanted to place a round orange peel on a flat surface; you would have to stretch the skin to accomplish it. The same is true of two-dimensional nautical charts that portray the round earth. The most common projection we are familiar with is the Mercator projection. This is your typical automobile road map. If you were to look at a nautical chart that displayed both New York and England and drew a line between the two points, your route would appear to be straight and the shortest, but in truth it would not be a great circle route. If you were to follow a great circle route on a Mercator projection chart, your initial route would diverge north of the line and the northerly deviation would increase until you were halfway there and then decrease until it met the drawn straight line in England. For the mariner to plot a great circle route, he would have to first plot a series of points on a different projection, called a gnomonic projection, label each point by latitude and longitude, transpose those points back to a Mercator chart, and then connect them to form a curved line north of the straight line to represent the great circle route from New York to England. Recreational boaters, however, traveling a short distance, generally did not have to worry about great circle routes. They could simply draw a line from A to B on the Mercator projection, since the deviation from the great circle route is minimal over a short distance.

The traditional paper nautical chart remains an excellent tool for navigation. It depicts the water depth, with different colors to warn of shallow water, and most important, the buoys that form part of the nautical buoy system that show safe passages. The most important buoys are red and green to show the safe course with indications of the flashing light patterns of each buoy, so navigation can be undertaken at night. All of this information now appears on electronic display at the helm of the yacht, guiding the mariner at every step.

Today, most boaters learn very little of navigational principles. While at one time, mariners would plot their courses on paper charts and measure the distances between points along the line as well as the intended compass direction (using a figure on the chart called a compass rose), today boaters typically mark a point on the electronic chart display much in the way a driver of a car does. Of course, if the power fails and all one is left with is the mechanical compass, which requires no electrical power, most boaters would simply be lost at sea.

When I began boating, the most advanced electronic navigation system, known as Loran-C, relatively crude by today's standards, was quite ingenious. Land-based radio antennas would transmit signals that created lobes that intersected. These lines and points of intersection would be depicted on the paper nautical chart, and numbers representing the boat's actual position would be displayed on the boater's receiving unit. This would accord the boater a fair degree of accuracy to determine the position of the boat. However, because of the effects of land masses varying the speed of the radio waves, the position fix could be as much as a quarter mile off—not much of a problem on the open sea, but a critical error when navigating a narrow harbor. Nautical chart makers began to compensate for this variation on later charts, with varying degrees of accuracy. On the other hand, if you got to a particular point or buoy and noted the actual numbers being displayed, you could achieve near-perfect "repeatable accuracy." Fishermen in particular would find this very useful because when they would discover a desirable fishing spot, they could note the numbers on the display and return to that precise spot another day.

With the advent of the global positioning system (GPS), everything changed. While at first the government deliberately degraded the accuracy of the system for recreational use (thinking it would hamper hostile military operations), eventually the government lifted this filter. Today, except in an unusual situation in which satellite signals are blocked, mariners can usually determine their position on earth within a few feet. Today, well-equipped mariners also have at their disposal not only the GPS-generated picture of their position but the added information provided by radar and AIS. Radar displays for many miles away the location and direction of movement of every boat as well as the reflections of buoys and other objects or obstructions, such as bridges or anchored boats. AIS broadcasts the identity, direction, and speed of all commercial boats and recreational boats that have the equipment aboard.

CHAPTER 21
A GHOST FROM THE PAST

Chadbourne & Parke was a distinguished law firm with a history dating back to 1902. Over the course of a century, it did the legal work for many American corporations, including the American Tobacco Company. But almost a century ago, it suffered a deep wound that left a scar. In 1939, Martin Manton, the Senior Circuit Judge of the United States Court of Appeals for the Second Circuit, was indicted and convicted of bribery. He had, among other crimes, accepted a bribe from a Chadbourne partner to influence a decision involving the American Tobacco Company. In the decades to follow, the incident faded into the dustbin of history.

In the early 1990s, Stuart Rosenthal was a partner in the real-estate department at the Chadbourne law firm. One day, federal agents came to the Chadbourne offices at Rockefeller Center and asked to see Rosenthal. He met the agents and was shocked by what they had to say. They told Rosenthal that they had a videotape of him gambling in a casino in Atlantic City. As most people know, casinos have extensive security, including "eye in the sky" cameras that are constantly monitored. According to the agents, Rosenthal had won $80,000 at the roulette table. He then took his chips and stuffed them into envelopes of just under $10,000 each and gave the envelopes to someone to exchange the chips for cash at the cashier's window. The agents intimated that unless Rosenthal cooperated, he would face indictment in a matter to be prosecuted by the Unites States Attorney in New Jersey. The potential crime was known as "structuring." Under federal law, it is a crime to assist a financial institution (which includes a casino) in avoiding its currency-reporting requirements that mandate it to report cash financial transactions of $10,000 or more.

At the time, Stanley Arkin, a well-known lawyer with a reputation for his aggressive defense of clients, was also a partner at the Chadbourne law firm. Rosenthal called him, and he joined the meeting with the federal agents, who played the videotape. Rosenthal's wife was a practicing lawyer. She and Arkin, coming to Rosenthal's defense, worked out a strategy. Arkin and an associate contacted the U.S. Attorney's office in New Jersey and eventually negotiated for Rosenthal to get a deferred prosecution agreement from the Justice Department in exchange for his cooperation in their investigation of gambling in Atlantic City. The federal prosecutors had made it clear that they intended to make an example of Rosenthal as a lawyer in a major firm who should have known better.

During the course of the government's investigation, the United States Supreme Court had decided a case on appeal from the United States Court of Appeals for the First Circuit: *Ratzlaf v. United States*, 510 U.S. 135 (1994). The high court held that the "structuring" statute required the government to prove what is known as a "specific intent" to violate the statute involved—a high burden.

As part of Rosenthal's efforts to coöperate, his plan took shape. He wore a wire recorder to return to Atlantic City to secure evidence against others who might be engaging in the same conduct. He also resigned from the Chadbourne law firm. Arkin and his associate drafted letters, edited by Rosenthal, for submission to the Justice Department to demonstrate that Rosenthal had already suffered by giving up his law partnership. At the end of more than a year, a number of indictments were returned against others who had allegedly engaged in structuring at Atlantic City casinos. Rosenthal got a pass.

After a criminal indictment no longer posed a threat to Rosenthal, he began making telephone calls to his former partners at the law firm, including its Chairman, with whom Rosenthal had had a good relationship. Secretly taping the telephone call, Rosenthal asked the Chairman, "Can you explain again why I was forced out of the firm?" During the conversation, the Chairman said, "Look, Stuart, understand that the firm had a sensitivity going back to the Judge Manton era." Armed with this recording, Rosenthal filed a lawsuit in state court in Manhattan, suing the law firm as well as its many individual partners—among them, the estate of Edmund Muskie, a former senator and candidate for Vice President of the United States. I was called in to represent the firm and its partners.

In his complaint, contrary to what he told the government to show his acceptance of responsibility, Rosenthal claimed that, in fact, he had never actually resigned from the firm but had been fired. As an alternative theory, he claimed that if in fact he had resigned, it was only because the firm pressured him, leaving him no alternative but to resign; according to Rosenthal, had he refused to resign, the firm would have called a partners' meeting to vote to cancel his partnership, which likely would have become public and made it impossible for him to be a stealth cooperator with the government. He claimed that by forcing his resignation, the firm violated its fiduciary duties to him.

As the bases for Rosenthal's claims became clear during the pretrial course of the litigation, he argued that the firm had overreacted due to its supposed sensitivity about the Manton affair and that the firm should have merely sidelined him temporarily, not expelled him. He bolstered his argument by asserting that in any event, he never would have been convicted of a crime, because in light of the Ratzlaf case requiring that the government show a defendant's "specific intent," he never could have been convicted. In his court complaint, Rosenthal sought millions of dollars in damages, calculated by factoring in the twenty-five years or so that he might have remained at the law firm while making large sums of money, and then, assuming that because of the firm's actions, he would be unable to make any significant money in the future. This was questionable as a matter of theory and fact, but our system allows many cases to go forward despite the apparent improbability of success, particularly if juries are to decide the issue.

The jury case was assigned to New York State Supreme Court Justice Herman Cahn, a Harvard Law–educated judge who was highly regarded for his intellect and fairness to litigants. Rosenthal was initially represented by a lawyer whose conduct at times was rude and unprofessional, leaving, at one point, Justice Cahn to assign a court-appointed Referee to be physically present during the course of the depositions to take place during the pretrial phase of the case.

Because Rosenthal's now ex-wife had counselled Rosenthal along with Arkin at the initial phase of Rosenthal's resignation from the firm and decision to cooperate with the government, I obtained Ms. Rosenthal's deposition, in part to see if she would confirm that she agreed with Arkin's advice that Rosenthal resign. In depositions, lawyers often ask exploratory questions of witnesses and occasionally stumble upon a gold mine. And here is where I got lucky. Taking a shot in the dark, I asked Ms. Rosenthal, "Did you ever accuse your husband of doing something immoral or illegal?" She replied, "Yes." I asked her to explain: "In my divorce complaint." At that point, I requested that the complaint (which had been filed in court under seal) be produced to me, which drew a predictable objection. I filed a written motion with the court for an order requiring the complaint's production, and my adversary filed a formal objection, saying the divorce complaint was irrelevant and should remain private. Justice Cahn ordered the document to be sent to him to be reviewed *in camera* (meaning, for his eyes only) and said he would decide the issue.

The retired judge who was designated to referee the contentious pretrial depositions found himself unexpectedly pleased with his assignment. In anticipation of trial, one of the evidentiary issues we faced was how to authenticate and get into evidence at trial the casino videotape that had been provided to us by the government. It showed Rosenthal, somewhat overweight, dressed in a gray sweatsuit into which he stuffed chips won at the roulette table, knowing he was violating the law. This evidence would tend to show that the likelihood of conviction was high. Through the auspices of the New Jersey courts, we obtained the deposition of the security director at the casino, hoping to have him authenticate the video tape. My colleague and I, accompanied by the Referee, drove down to Atlantic City, booked rooms at the hotel, and enjoyed our evening at the casino in question. The next day, we showed up at the casino security office, got a tour of the operation, and took the deposition testimony of the head of security, who authenticated the tape. The retired judge had stayed in the casino long after we left to turn in for the night. I am sure this was among his best assignments.

There was one other important item we needed to tie down before trial. We had spoken with the Assistant United States Attorney in New Jersey who had overseen the investigation and prosecution of the casino cases. He expressed outrage that Rosenthal was contending that he had never actually resigned from the law firm; he recalled that the heart of Rosenthal's "pitch" to the government was that he had already suffered enough by his resignation. The prosecutor said he would be happy to testify to that effect, provided that we could get clearance from the Justice Department for him to testify. We ultimately did, and we took his deposition for use at trial.

Two more years went by, and the case was finally scheduled for trial before a jury. Two days before the scheduled trial, a new lawyer for Rosenthal appeared with me in the jury part of the Court to conduct a voir dire of juror candidates. As is the custom in New York (discussed elsewhere in this book), New York state court judges do not ordinarily conduct the voir dire in civil cases, or are even present, leaving lawyers to fend for themselves, who often find themselves in disputes about the proper questioning. That is exactly what happened here.

Under the applicable rules for questioning of prospective jurors, lawyers are permitted to explain their contentions, to allow them to ascertain if a potential juror can be fair and impartial in that particular case. In telling my version of events, I mentioned that Rosenthal taped a phone call with the Chairman of the firm. My adversary lawyer jumped up and objected and asked to see a judicial hearing officer down the hall who had been designated to address any jury-selection issues. He demanded—and the hearing officer agreed—that the prospective jurors be instructed that it is not illegal in New York State for one party to record a telephone conversation. Ultimately a panel of seven jurors and two alternates was chosen to hear the trial.

There was one more step before the actual trial. As is usual, we met with the judge to discuss the trial procedures to be followed. We sat down with Justice Cahn in the courtroom anteroom. He began by telling us that he had recently been tidying up his chambers and found an envelope that had slipped between his desk and the wall. The envelope contained Ms. Rosenthal's divorce complaint that had been the subject of the motion two years before, which had never been decided by the judge. The judge turned to my adversary and said, "What I have seen in this divorce complaint is despicable. Counsel, if you do anything to have witnesses bolster Mr. Rosenthal's character, I will give this complaint to Mr. Zauderer to use for cross-examination of Mr. Rosenthal."

The conference soon ended, and we had about an hour before the jury was sworn and the trial commenced. My adversary rushed into an empty room and frantically began to strike out from his notes many of the questions he had planned to ask of witnesses who were prepared to testify that Mr. Rosenthal had a good reputation in his community. Among others he was counting on was the rabbi of Rosenthal's synagogue. Given the judge's ruling, he could not come to Rosenthal's assistance without being cross-examined by me with the divorce complaint in hand.

Near the end of the trial, Mr. Rosenthal's counsel decided to "give up" if Chadbourne would pay a relatively small amount, at least sufficient to pay part of Rosenthal's legal bills. Chadbourne agreed to do so, on one condition: that the relatively small sum *not* be secret; rather the number should be published, which it was. This was quite unusual and clever, as the firm did not want people in the community to speculate that the firm had paid some large amount of money to end the litigation.

After leaving the courthouse, I never saw Mr. Rosenthal or his lawyer again. That was a quarter century ago. I heard later that Mr. Rosenthal had committed suicide.

CHAPTER 22

MEETING THE PRESS

Although I thought that my experience on the radio might give me some advantage in a courtroom, it never occurred to me that it would also serve me well in interacting with television and print media. In my law practice, I have observed that lawyers are often uncomfortable in responding to reporters' inquiries about their own cases or legal topics generally. They seem to be almost paralyzed by the thought of saying something wrong. Another common handicap I have observed is their inability, when asked about a legal issue, to explain it in a way that would be understandable and meaningful to the public.

It was the practice of the New York State Bar Association to provide a day of media training to newly elected chairs of each Section of the Association. As the incoming Chair of the Commercial and Federal Litigation Section almost thirty years ago, I attended one of these sessions. The staff thought responding to mock press inquiries came easy to me, so they designated me to respond to press inquiries about legal matters, such as high-profile trials. While reporters at major newspapers and television stations in urban areas typically have their own sources, reporters employed by small-town newspapers and local television stations—many of them at their first journalism jobs—have no experience in the legal world. Not knowing where to turn, they will call the Bar Association, which will refer the inquiring reporter to a member. I would frequently get these calls and would speak with the reporters or appear for a television interview. In today's world, when you give an interview to a major newspaper or are interviewed on television, your comments are instantly seen live or on the internet by many in the media who are interested in the same topic. So, beginning with the exposure I received almost thirty years ago, my name began to appear more and more in the Rolodexes of reporters and television anchors.

I live in Westchester County in New York State. About twenty years ago, I experienced some back pain and began to see a local chiropractor. One day, as I was waiting to be seen, a distinguished-looking older man sitting near me started a conversation. He was an American historian whose book about great historical documents entitled *A Documentary History of the United States* had been on the reading list in my political science course at Union College decades before. Richard Heffner, the author, had also been a pioneer in public television, having served as the first president of the public television station Channel 13 in New York City. Also, in the 1960s, on behalf of the broadcasting industry, he had served as the person who assigns industry ratings to movies to alert the audience to scenes of sex. As he later explained it with a chuckle, each month he flew from New York to Los Angeles and viewed the "dirty movies" that earned either an *R* rating or *X* rating. He told me that the industry itself had created this rating system in an effort to stave off intervention by

Congress, which they feared would begin to regulate the content of sex in the movies.

My encounter with Heffner led to almost a decade of deeply gratifying experiences with him. He was the host of the PBS Television program *The Open Mind*, the oldest interview show on public television. He would tape half-hour interviews with interesting people—many of them world figures—that would be shown initially on public television in New York City and then distributed to public television stations throughout the country. Columbia University has a center devoted to Heffner's programs, which are archived there and can be viewed today on the internet. Over the years, Heffner conducted eight half-hour interviews of me, on the subjects of "The Jury System on Trial"; "Forcing Lawyers to Retire…an Age-Old or Just an Old Age Problem?"; "The Law…Fitting a Profession into 'the Business Model'"; "On Lawyers, Judges, and Justice in America"; "The Legal Brain-Scape: Neuroscience and the Law"; "A New York Times Editorial, 5/7/2012: 'The Cautionary Tale of Dewey & LeBoeuf'"; "A Newer Look at Cameras in the Courts," and "In the Name of the Law…." You can view these programs if you search online for "Mark Zauderer The Open Mind."

Heffner was perhaps the best interviewer I have encountered. He would probe but asked open-ended questions that would allow his subject time to develop his or her thoughts. He always seemed to have a follow-up question that would permit even more in-depth exploration of the subject at hand. From time to time, Heffner would come down to lower Manhattan, where my law office was at the time, and join me for an extended lunch. More than once, he enjoyed telling me about his background, including the fact that his father was a bookie and that it was only by chance that he, his son, ended up a professor, a historian, and a television host.

My many interviews in the print and television media have been enjoyable. From time to time, even when I have been expected to speak about very familiar issues, the exercise has required me to do a deep dive into these areas so as to satisfy myself that my commentary is accurate. I have also enjoyed receiving emails from strangers expressing their views on my commentary and, on occasion, heard from people in my past with whom I had lost touch. In several instances, my personal acquaintances were renewed as a result of these media appearances.

CHAPTER 23

THE ROBBER BARON AND HIS GRANDSON

Among the notable "robber barons" of the second half of the nineteenth century was James Jewett Stillman. He was a major investor in land, banking, and railroads and a founder of National City Bank, along with the Rockefeller family and Standard Oil. By the 1890s, the bank was the largest in the United States. The Stillman and Rockefeller families were joined in a number of marriages, whose descendants bear their names today. James Stillman died in 1918 leaving a fortune that he bequeathed in trust to his several children. The beneficiaries of that fortune would continue to enjoy the income from that trust from generation to generation.

In 1984, a colleague of mine called to say I would be contacted by a man named Calvin Stillman. A few minutes later, that call came and Mr. Stillman, just several blocks away from my office, came up to see me. Meeting him at reception, I saw a tall, patrician figure. His English seemed to be flat American with a tinge of an English accent—sort of reminiscent of those 1930s black-and-white movies in which the American actors speak with just enough affect to let us know that their ancestors were British.

Like many of his family members, Calvin Stillman was a graduate of Harvard, where a building bore the family name. But Stillman was somewhat of a black sheep in the family. He was the only Democrat in a family of staunch Republicans. He had given away a substantial part of his assets, including a large tract of land near Storm King Mountain in the Hudson Valley of New York, and he was a passionate environmentalist before it became a mainstream trend. Stillman told me how he had been raised in a double townhouse on East 72nd Street in Manhattan (which is now the Lycée Français school). At dinner, there was a footman behind every chair, while his father, Guy Stillman, presided over the family dinner. During World War II, rather than avail himself of family connections and secure a position as an officer, Cal enlisted in the army as a private and was sent abroad to Europe. To me, he closely resembled the wealthy Adlai Stevenson, who, more than once, was spotted with a hole in the sole of his shoe when he ran for President.

Like many wealthy people, Cal had put his financial affairs in the hands of a New York City lawyer, a partner in a small law firm. The lawyer oversaw a "housekeeping trust" to pay Cal's ordinary bills and also had control over a personal foundation that Cal had set up to make annual gifts to various needy persons or small organizations. Just two days before he came to see me, the law firm had called Cal and asked him to come to their office. There, the managing partner explained to Cal that his law partner had disbursed Cal's trust funds to himself and to various friends in strange investment schemes. To add to that, the partners in the law firm had taken loans from Cal's trust that had not been paid back. My colleague, the outside lawyer for the law firm, had walked Cal into the office of the Disciplinary

Committee to report the lawyer's actions. The staff lawyer for the Disciplinary Committee told Cal to get his own lawyer. That is when the law firm's outside lawyer called to introduce me to Cal.

These events caused problems for Cal on a number of fronts. Of course, first and foremost, we had to try to get compensation for the financial diversions. Seeking recompense from the lawyer who had stolen the money would have been a fool's errand. In fact, it was rumored that the lawyer had acquired a cocaine habit, and after the matter was reported to the Disciplinary Committee, he was quickly suspended from his law practice. The second problem we had to address was the fact that Cal's small foundation, of which he was a trustee, had suffered a loss of most of its principal as a result of the lawyer's actions. That could result in Cal having personal liability for the lost funds. We had to deal with the Charities Bureau of the New York Attorney General's office on that problem, as well as the Internal Revenue Service. The third area that I felt needed attention was getting Cal back on a solid footing and establishing a corps of advisors to assist him with financial management and estate planning.

Under the James Stillman 1918 Trust, beneficiaries such as Cal had the ability to request an invasion of principal for certain needs. Given the losses occasioned by the lawyer's thefts, we succeeded on several occasions in persuading the trustees, the Bank of New York and a partner at Paul Weiss, to make a distribution of principal to Cal. Our second effort was prompted by the fact that Cal had no natural children but maintained a close relationship with the two daughters of a prior marriage. So, we considered the possibility of Cal adopting his two adult stepdaughters so that upon Cal's passing, the income from his share of the trust would benefit them; were he to leave no children, the principal of the trust would be transferred to trusts in the other lines that descended from James Stillman. In researching whether adoption would achieve Cal's purpose, we found that in 1918 when the trust was created, a testator who gave rights to children as remaindermen of trusts was not deemed to include *adopted* children unless the legal instrument specifically provided for that. The New York Legislature changed that in 1963, but the change did not apply retroactively to trusts created before that time, so we had to abandon that idea. However, in discussing Cal's estate plan, he made it very clear that, unlike many people who would want to give advance authorization to have their life support discontinued if they were in a coma or suffering, he wished to have the life support continued as long as possible, even if he was suffering, so that the income from the trust would continue to flow as long as possible for the benefit of his wife, Doris.

In order to obtain compensation for the lawyer's perfidious actions, I brought a lawsuit in federal court in Manhattan on behalf of Cal against his law firm. After some initial discovery, in addition to its litigation counsel, the law firm retained retired Court of Appeals Judge Jacob Fuchsberg to approach me to explore settlement. After quite a bit of back and forth, we were able to achieve a settlement that largely restored the funds that had been stolen and squandered.

In the thirty years that followed, I maintained a close relationship with Cal and Doris and for decades served as a trustee of trusts they created. They moved to St. Petersburg, Florida, and enjoyed a peaceful, modest life, where I would visit them at least quarterly to ensure they were being properly cared for. Cal died in 2013 at the age of ninety-seven; Doris died several years thereafter. I felt privileged to have known and served these two individuals. Their charitable spirit has inspired me to "give back" to those who are deserving of help.

The author with his father, Jerome Zauderer.

The author with his mother, Dorothy Zauderer.

The author's seventh grade class with actor James Cagney, filming *Never Steal Anything Small.*

The author's mother, Dorothy.

The author as a student at Union College.

The author at the helm of his yacht, *Different Drummer,* with then US Attorney General Loretta Lynch at the helm.

Yacht *Different Drummer* at rest.

The author with President Barack Obama.

The author and his friend Danny with Brooklyn Dodgers star pitcher Johnny Podres.

Three of five FBI agents providing security for the Attorney General on *Different Drummer*.

The author at court on a high-profile case.

Cover of *Fortune* magazine featuring an article about the author.

The author's Lawyers Who Lead by Example Award conferred in 2015 by the *New York Law Journal.*

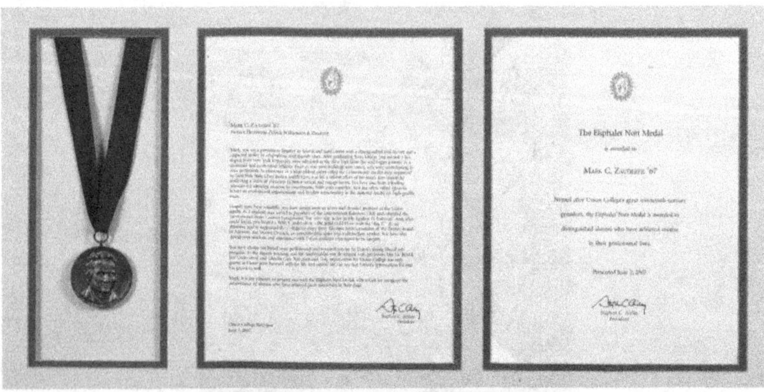

The Eliphalet Nott Medal conferred for alumni achievement by the author's alma mater, Union College.

The author during one of his nine interviews on the PBS television series *The Open Mind*.

The author receiving an honorary Doctor of Laws degree after giving the 2016 commencement day speech at Touro Law School.

The author with Anthony Marshall, the son of Brooke Astor.

The author in a recent photo.

CHAPTER 24
A WIDOW'S REMORSE

In the post–World War II era, real estate in New York City experienced a boom. Two of the major real-estate players in New York City were Seymour Cohn and his brother Sylvan Lawrence. Between them, they owned or managed more than one hundred office buildings in Manhattan, a vast empire producing a fortune in revenues. Sylvan was married to Alice Lawrence, with whom he had an unhappy relationship. In 1981, Sylvan died, and his brother Seymour became the executor of Sylvan's estate. Mrs. Lawrence went to war with Seymour over a twenty-five-year period. She was represented by a small, well-respected law firm known as Graubard Miller. Over this period, the law firm represented her in continuous contentious litigation in the Surrogate's Court in Manhattan. At one point, her lawyers had succeeded in forcing Seymour to sell off estate properties or interests, yielding her personally over $350 million in addition to other recoveries from the estate.

Mrs. Lawrence was sometimes compared to the notorious Leona Helmsley, who while running her late husband's real-estate empire, was often referred to as "the Queen of Mean." Mrs. Helmsley was also known for her generous use of profanity and cold-hearted treatment of employees. This characterization seemed to fit Mrs. Lawrence to a *T*.

In January 2005, Mrs. Lawrence wanted to change her fee arrangement with the Graubard law firm. She pointed out that she had paid the firm more than $20 million since the early 1980s and wanted the firm to "be my partner." As she had many litigation claims against Seymour Cohn that were still unresolved—and no one knew how much effort and time would ultimately be required to litigate those claims—she asked the firm to switch to a new fee arrangement, with a contingency portion the most significant component. With the advice of her accountant, Mrs. Lawrence signed an agreement that provided for four quarterly payments to the Graubard law firm of $300,000 plus 40 percent of any future recoveries in the ongoing litigation against Sylvan's and Seymour's estates. Graubard was reluctant to take the risk of a contingency-fee arrangement, but it did so since Mrfos. Lawrence was probably the firm's most important client.

The customary process of document discovery continued in the Surrogate's Court litigation. A few months later, the lawyer for the Cohn estate called the Graubard lawyers and asked for a meeting. They met in a conference room, where the Cohn estate's lawyers produced a folder of documents that proved to be a "smoking gun." They showed that Seymour, while acting as the executor of Sylvan's estate, had secretly sold estate properties to offshore trusts that he controlled and, in violation of his fiduciary duties to Sylvan's estate and Mrs. Lawrence as a beneficiary, had pocketed the funds for his own benefit. With this information now disclosed, the case quickly settled for a payment to Mrs. Lawrence of $110 million. Ironically, this was only the beginning of a different war.

With the $110 million settlement signed and sealed, Graubard wrote to their client, Mrs. Lawrence, requesting payment of the 40 percent contingency fee, amounting to about $44 million. Unbeknownst to Graubard, Mrs. Lawrence had retained another lawyer just before the $110 million settlement was paid to her, who wrote back to Graubard on her behalf refusing to pay the contingency fee, claiming it was unconscionably high, in violation of attorney ethical rules. It was not so much the precise percentage of 40 percent that was likely the basis of the challenge. Applicable ethics rules require any legal fee to be "reasonable." When judging whether a fee is reasonable, courts look to a number of factors. Here, Mrs. Lawrence would be pointing to the fact that the amount of lawyer time spent on the matter between the signing of January 2005 revised engagement letter and the date of the settlement several months later would translate into an equivalent to $11,000 an hour for the attorneys' time.

Graubard retained me to represent it. We pursued a lawsuit in the Surrogate's Court in Manhattan and claimed the $40 million–plus fee. Mrs. Lawrence's response to the complaint was quite a surprise. Not only did she allege that the contingency fee was unconscionable, but she said that in 1998, unbeknownst to the rest of the partners at the Graubard firm, the three partners who had represented her over the many years had requested that she pay them personally $5 million as gifts, which she did. In addition, the following year she paid them personally an additional $3 million to reimburse them for their payment of the federal gift taxes on the gifts. When the tabloids got hold of this, headlines screamed in bold type how so-called greedy lawyers had taken advantage of a poor widow.

In the Surrogate's Court where this case was to be tried, it is customary for that busy court to appoint a lawyer or a retired judge to oversee pretrial matters, conduct the trial, and make a report to the Surrogate. The Surrogate, in turn, can either accept, reject, or modify the findings. The court appointed a distinguished retired Associate Judge of the New York Court of Appeals, Howard Levine, to hear the matter as a so-called Referee.

As the pretrial phase of the case began, we sought to take the deposition of Mrs. Lawrence as soon as possible, because she was well advanced in years, and we did not want to risk losing the opportunity to question her. However, Mrs. Lawrence's lawyer persuaded Judge Levine to put off her deposition, arguing that the 40 percent fee was unconscionable on its face and that the case did not warrant factual development. Judge Levine granted their request to postpone Mrs. Lawrence's deposition. The issue of unconscionability worked its way through the court system for several years. First, Judge Levine ruled that the legal issue could not be decided simply on the face of the 40 percent fee agreement and denied Mrs. Lawrence's motion to dismiss it. That decision was affirmed by the Surrogate. Mrs. Lawrence then took an appeal to the Appellate Division, First Department. The majority of that Court affirmed the denial of Mrs. Lawrence's motion, with one judge issuing a stinging dissent, arguing that the fee agreement was unconscionable on its face. New York's highest court, the Court of Appeals, agreed to hear the case (that Court, like the U.S. Supreme Court, historically grants the right to appeal in only a small percentage of cases). On the oral argument, I encountered vigorous questioning by the judges, who, among other issues that interested them, pressed me hard on what they should hold is the boundary between reasonable and unconscionable fee agreements. My arguments ultimately prevailed, as the Court rejected Mrs. Lawrence's argument that the fee agreement was unconscionable on its face, and held that the matter would be remanded to Judge Levine for pretrial and ultimately trial proceedings.

Mrs. Lawrence's lawyers then pulled out every stop to delay her deposition, citing one excuse after another. Then one day they suddenly announced that Mrs. Lawrence had died. Judge Levine, it appeared, was quite upset with the conduct of Mrs. Lawrence's lawyers and, on our motion, made some important evidentiary rulings that would apply to the trial that would severely hamper Mrs. Lawrence's case.

One of the factors a court considers in determining whether a fee arrangement is "reasonable" is what the lawyer and client would have expected to be the future course of the litigation at the time they made the fee arrangement. For example, let's say the lawyer asks for an agreement on a 40 percent contingency when the lawyer knew a settlement had already been agreed to and was likely to be finalized shortly. In that circumstance, a court might find the contingency fee to be unreasonable. On the other hand, in a commercial matter, if the time and effort anticipated to conclusion might be very substantial as viewed at the time, a 40 percent fee would most certainly be considered to be reasonable. In January 2005, when Mrs. Lawrence requested the fee modification, everyone involved thought that the litigations against the Seymour Cohn estate, which involved many different claims, would likely continue for many years, considering the trials and appeals that would be forthcoming.

When the matter finally came to trial before Judge Levine, the defense intended to call as an expert witness a law professor who was a respected expert on ethics issues, to offer the opinion that Graubard's fees were excessive and unreasonable when viewed from the perspective of the lawyer and client in January 2005 when the revised fee agreement was made. Under applicable court rules, expert witnesses are required to provide in advance some basic information about the substance of their opinion to which they will be testifying. In preparing to testify, an expert witness typically spends days and weeks, particularly in a high-value case, combing the record of the litigation, reading not only the pleadings but the many relevant documents, deposition transcripts, and briefs submitted in the course of the years of litigation, as well as prior decisions in the case—all to bolster the expert's credibility when his or her opinion is given at trial. In this case, perhaps because the expert did not have the time to devote to it, or the Lawrence estate did not want to pay for it, the expert considered only an "assumed set of facts" prepared and given to him by Mrs. Lawrence's counsel. These facts assumed the truth of the version of facts being asserted by Graubard. The professor would then testify that even assuming these facts to be true, Graubard's fee was unreasonable.

Before trial, I wanted to be sure that in fact the witness had not reviewed any other materials in the litigations and that I could be certain that the assumed facts were all that he reviewed and had no further familiarity with all of the relevant circumstances. Accordingly, I issued a trial subpoena to the expert requiring him to bring to court on the day of his testimony any document he had reviewed in formulating his testimony, besides the statement of assumed facts. He appeared in court with a small knapsack, which he gave to my associate, saying it contained whatever he had reviewed. My associate looked inside and confirmed to me that there was nothing except the document with the assumed facts upon which he based his testimony.

When called to the stand by Mrs. Lawrence's attorneys, the ethics expert gave the anticipated testimony. He explained that on the "assumed facts," in his opinion, the 40 percent contingency fee was unreasonable and unconscionable. He finished his testimony just before the lunch break, with cross-examination to begin immediately after the lunch break.

During the course of the litigation, Graubard had provided me a copy of a letter, written almost a decade before, when the fee dispute had first arisen, that the professor had written to one of the partners at Graubard in response to a request that he have a consultation about the fee matter. He wrote, in substance, that he could not give an opinion on the reasonableness of the fee without knowing all of the details of the case.

It was clear that Mrs. Lawrence's counsel as well as the professor were unaware of the letter. Before showing it to the witness, I asked the professor on the witness stand, "Isn't it true that one cannot give an opinion about the reasonableness of a legal fee without knowing all the details of the case?" Rather than agree with me, he gave an answer that was not responsive to the question. I asked it again and he gave pretty much the same answer. I then gave him a copy of the letter, handing a copy to him and to the judge, as well as opposing counsel. And then I asked the witness, "Is that your signature that appears on this letter?" Mrs. Lawrence's counsel jumped up and objected. He said we never had told the opposing counsel that we intended to use the letter at trial. Judge Levine said, "Overruled; this is cross-examination. Plaintiff was not required to produce that document in advance of trial."

I followed up with question after question to the witness about each of Mr. Lawrence's claims that still needed to be litigated going forward from January 2005, when the modified fee arrangement was made. This went on painfully for what must have seemed like an eternity, as I asked the witness about the details of each claim, including what was alleged; what the defenses were; and how much work did he think would be involved by the Graubard firm going forward. He had no idea about any of those details, so he obviously was not in a position to evaluate the critical issue of how much time and effort remained for these claims to be litigated. After about twenty minutes of this line of questioning, Judge Levine interrupted, "I get the point." The witness was excused.

Following the trial, Judge Levine issued a report recommending, among other things, that the contingency fee owed to the Graubard firm be reduced from $44 million to approximately $15.8 million. The parties then filed various motions and cross-motions in the Surrogate's Court to confirm, modify, or reject Judge Levine's report. The Surrogate's Court confirmed that portion of the report, approving Judge Levine's recommendation of a $15.8 million fee as essentially a "middle-ground remedy" that recognized that the revised retainer agreement was not unconscionable at the outset, but would have become unconscionable if enforced according to its terms. On appeal, the Appellate Division held that the revised retainer agreement was both procedurally and substantively unconscionable, and that the $44 million fee was disproportionate to the value of the services rendered. However, rather than permit Graubard to receive a reduced $15.8 million contingency fee, the Appellate Division went further and found that the law firm should be awarded a fee equal to the amount it would have received under the original hourly fee agreement—a much smaller number than Judge Levine's recommendation of $15.8 million.

For the second time, we found ourselves in the New York Court of Appeals in Albany. This was unusual, given that leave to appeal to that court is granted in only a small percentage of cases in which it is sought, and that high court would hear the case a second time was virtually unheard-of. (Coincidentally, within the past year, I argued another case for the second time in the Court of Appeals.) At this point, after nine years of litigation, the financial toll of the litigation led the Graubard firm to retain a highly respected lawyer, Brian Shoot, who would not be charging them on an hourly-time basis, to handle this final appeal. But they hoped I could participate with him in the oral argument before the Court after the briefs were written. Accordingly, I made an agreement with the firm that Shoot would write to the Court, asking the seven judges to allow me to participate in the oral argument; but if they did not, I would earn a contingency fee if the appeal succeeded, as long as I sat at the counsel table to be able to consult with Shoot during the argument.

As it turned out, the Court allowed me to participate in the oral argument. In the course of the argument, Judge Victoria Graffeo asked me how the Court, in its decision, could explain to the public such an extraordinary legal fee in light of the time expended. I replied that the contingency-fee system is the key to the courthouse for most people. Turning to other lawyers in the courtroom, I asked, if one of my colleagues engaged me on a time basis to handle a litigation, how would he react when I said, "Don't worry, maybe we will get through the first motion for only twenty-five thousand dollars; we'll see what happens after that." I added, "Who can afford to pay hundreds of thousands of dollars to a lawyer in a litigation that, with trials and appeals, can go on for years?"

Another judge asked, "How can you justify a fee that would amount to eleven thousand dollars per hour?" I explained that the question contains a false premise: that the client is buying the lawyer's time. I added that in a time-based fee arrangement, the lawyer is paid but the client takes the risk of an unsuccessful result. In contrast, in a contingency arrangement, the lawyer takes a risk, and the interests of the client and the lawyer are aligned: the client wants the best result possible in as short a period of time as possible. Would the contingency fee involved here be more reasonable if the lawyer took more time to obtain a lesser result?

On October 28, 2014, the New York Court of Appeals came down with a stunning decision. It reversed the Appellate Division decision, which had reduced Graubard's fee to what it would have been under the original hourly fee agreement, and allowed the entire $44 million-plus fee, which, with statutory interest at 9 percent for a year, brought the total amount to over $87 million. There were no more avenues of appeal. Since interest on the total amount would run at 9 percent per year, each day that passed, the amount due would grow about $21,000 per day. Within days, payment was made, and the case was over. My small percentage contingency fee on the $87 million award was certainly well worth my day trip to Albany.

CHAPTER 25

LEARNING ABOUT POLITICS

I had no involvement in politics for much of my life, other than as a ten-year-old. I sat on a soap box on Montague Street in Brooklyn Heights with my friend and a coffee can, soliciting contributions for the 1956 presidential election. "I'm for Adlai and Estes" read our sign. Running against President Dwight D. Eisenhower and Vice President Richard M. Nixon were Adlai Stevenson and Estes Kefauver. Party officials made us stop, and the item was reported as filler in the *Brooklyn Heights Press*. A decade later, as a student at Union College in Schenectady, I was recruited to join a small group at the Albany airport to greet Robert F. Kennedy as he disembarked an airplane while running for Senate in New York. Later, I received a signed thank-you note from RFK addressed to me with the spelling of my name garbled.

In 2006, I received a telephone call in my office from Andrew Cuomo, who asked if he could come up to see me. I knew little about him, other than that he had been secretary of HUD during the Clinton Administration. Based on what I knew of these kinds of visits, I assumed he would be arriving with a campaign finance person to ask for a check. It was a warm day in the summer. Cuomo planned to run in the fall against Jeanine Pirro to be Attorney General of the State of New York. He arrived at my office downtown by himself, to my surprise. We walked into my corner office on the thirty-fifth floor overlooking the Hudson River and the site of the destroyed World Trade Center Towers. Cuomo stood there for several minutes looking out and not saying anything. He then told me that he wanted to know my ideas about what issues he should focus on for his campaign. I wondered why he wanted to know my views. Only later did it become clear to me that my name had probably been given to him by a lawyer I knew with whom he had a close relationship. Connecting the dots, I thought that while he had a solid relationship with important people in the real-estate industry, even though he was a lawyer, he was probably looking to expand his reach in the legal community and was contacting a number of lawyers he thought had important connections.

Cuomo remained in my office for almost two hours. He floated the idea of focusing on corruption on Wall Street, but it became clear in our conversation that the subject was a centerpiece of Eliot Spitzer's upcoming campaign for Governor that fall. It was Spitzer's position as Attorney General that Cuomo was seeking to fill as Spitzer sought the governorship. Much of the remaining conversation centered on two subjects: the antique clocks in my office and boats.

I was impressed with Cuomo. Following our meeting, I joined a small group of lawyers who were assisting in his campaign. One of the experiences I was grateful for was working with Andrew's father, former Governor Mario Cuomo, in preparing Andrew for his upcoming debate with Jeanine Pirro. Following Andrew's election as Attorney General, he appointed me to serve as a member of a Judicial Screening Committee that recommends to the Governor judicial candidates who wanted to be elevated from the Supreme Court (a trial court) to the Appellate Division.

Several years later, a major university in New York was experiencing a financial crisis. Added to the usual financial pressures that any university faces was the unfortunate circumstance that the university had invested in a popular financial instrument, then known as an auction-rate security, that had been promoted by two major brokerages. But investors found that they had no market into which they could sell those securities. The Attorney General's office responded to investors' complaints and reached a settlement with the brokerages for them to buy back the securities. When the university sought to sell back its securities, the brokerages refused, claiming that because the university was a sophisticated investor, it was not entitled to relief under the terms of the Attorney General's settlement. If the university could not recover its investment, it faced an imminent financial collapse.

The university retained me, and before commencing a lawsuit, I reached out to counsel for one of the brokerage houses. In essence, I was told to "take a hike." That day was Christmas Eve. I called Cuomo's office and asked to speak to him, but he had already left. However, he called me back within the hour. I explained that I believed that the brokerage house was covered by the terms of the settlement and that unless something could be done about it, this not-for-profit university would be in a serious financial crisis. In New York, the Attorney General is the regulator of not-for-profit entities and exercises responsibilities to protect them. Cuomo said he would have someone call me back Monday morning. Sure enough, on Monday I received a call from the top financial regulator. I explained the situation in detail, and he said he would get back to me. On Thursday, I received a call from a lawyer from one of the brokerage houses. He said, very politely, "Mr. Zauderer, we are sending over to your office a check for twenty-seven million dollars." I received the check and turned it over to my client. I only wished that every representation could be that easy.

My contact with Mario Cuomo did not end with his son's campaign for Attorney General. The next year, when I was President of the Federal Bar Council, our organization bestowed its Public Service Award on Mario Cuomo at its Thanksgiving luncheon at the Waldorf Astoria. This is the largest lawyer/federal judge event in New York City, a tradition that has been in place for many decades. Although former Governor Cuomo had been given awards and spoken on hundreds of occasions, this event was important to him because it had been a long time since he had spoken to such a large crowd of lawyers and judges. In the weeks before the event, Cuomo called me a number of times to read me passages from his draft speech, asking my opinion on both tone and content. He also made a point of inquiring about my own career, leading him to be the first person to suggest that I write a memoir. Little did I know that I would follow his suggestion decades later.

At the Thanksgiving luncheon, Mario Cuomo gave a magnificent speech—a little bit of history, some humor, and some memorable thoughts for the audience to contemplate. In 1993, it was reported that Cuomo had declined a Supreme Court nomination offered by President Bill Clinton. Before he passed away, I asked him about that. He said he just could not see himself giving up the freedom of a public lifestyle. I can well understand why he would have been chosen.

CHAPTER 26

FROM RUSSIA—WITHOUT LOVE

In the years immediately after the collapse of the Soviet Union in 1991, the world began to take advantage of opportunities to do business in Russia and invest in Russia's economy. Among those who followed the trend were American law firms that stood ready to assist these businesses. One of these was Chadbourne & Parke, which opened an office in Moscow. In the late 1990s, Boris Yeltsin, the President of Russia, issued a decree that allowed private investment in Russian assets, including major industries such as Gazprom, the giant Russian energy company. But the institutional purchasers wishing to purchase shares in these industries had to have a significant ownership interest by Russians. A large Austrian bank, Creditanstalt, set up a start-up securities operation in Moscow with the requisite partial Russian ownership. The Austrian bank had consulted the Moscow office of Chadbourne to obtain legal advice concerning the legitimacy of this operation under Russian law. With its usual care, Chadbourne gave its advice with important caveats and qualifications.

Although shares of Gazprom were available in equivalents in foreign markets, the market price of the share equivalents was substantially higher than the price of those shares available to qualified Russian purchasers in Russia. The new securities operation took advantage of this price differential and purchased millions of Gazprom shares in Russia. One day, the Russian tax police raided the firm's offices in Moscow. Wearing masks and armed with automatic rifles, they shut down the firm and seized all of its records. Creditanstalt, the chief investor in this operation, brought a lawsuit in Supreme Court in New York against Chadbourne, seeking to recover its losses, claimed to be over $500 million. The bank alleged that it had followed Chadbourne's supposedly faulty legal advice in setting up the securities operation that led to the tax-police raid.

Once again, Chadbourne asked me to represent the firm. The case went on for over five years. Since many of the witnesses to relevant events were located in Eastern Europe and Russia, I enlisted the help of a colleague at my law firm, Daniel Rothstein, who was bilingual in English and Russian. In fact, both before and after the collapse of the Soviet Union, he had spent time working as a lawyer in Russia. When we would visit Moscow, sometimes for a day and other times for over a week, I never went anywhere without him at my side, since English was not widely spoken on the streets in Moscow, and I certainly could not read signs in the Russian alphabet.

Before traveling to Moscow, we were given a lead and learned of a "mole" in Austria who supposedly knew of the circumstances of the tax-police raid. Rothstein and I contacted him and flew to Vienna to debrief him. He believed that the tax-police raid was the result of an inside job that had been orchestrated by an employee of the securities firm who stole millions of Gazprom shares and had alerted the tax police to cover his tracks. We hoped to substantiate this and prove that even if Chadbourne's advice was off the mark—which it was not—it was this surreptitious action that was the cause of the loss, not Chadbourne's advice. But we know this would require hard work.

Arriving in Moscow for the first time, I did not feel as though I had arrived in a friendly place. The tone was set when I was met at the airport by an armed driver who had been designated to escort me to the law firm and any other places I needed to visit. While we undertook efforts to find documentation that might confirm the circumstances of the tax-police raid, we simultaneously took depositions in, among other places, Vienna, Bratislava, Budapest, and Russia. As if to confirm the sense of unease we experienced in Moscow, at one of the depositions, the stenographer suddenly stopped and appeared extremely anxious. For whatever reason, she expressed fear that she was being watched by Russian authorities for her participation in this deposition. With some difficulty, we persuaded her to continue.

In a malpractice case in which the adequacy of legal representation is questioned by the plaintiff, it is common to have expert witnesses on each side give their opinion as to the adequacy of the legal services provided. We consulted in Moscow with one of the leading lawyers in Russia, Sergei Magnitsky, who was prepared to give us an opinion favorable to our client. As the world learned, he was later imprisoned by Russian authorities and ultimately died under mysterious circumstances, supposedly from natural causes. The United States Congress passed a law, known as the Magnitsky Act, which imposed sanctions on Russian officials who shared responsibility for Magnitsky's imprisonment and death. This circumstance posed a substantial problem in our litigation. It was getting close to the time of trial, and we would have to find a new expert who would be supportive of our position. Given the unfolding political events in Russia, it was not at all clear that we could do that.

Fortunately, we were at last given access in Europe to a trove of documents that proved the inside job chain of events. At the end of the discovery phase of the case, we made a motion for summary judgment, which was ultimately granted by the trial court. Creditanstalt, which by then had merged into Bank Austria, took an appeal to the Appellate Division, which affirmed the trial court's dismissal of the case against Chadbourne. The bank attempted to appeal the case to the New York Court of Appeals, which refused to review it.

The pretrial discovery process in this case took me to other interesting places and exposed me to unexpected experiences, since witnesses to the relevant events were scattered throughout Eastern Europe. In Budapest, I went through the necessary international applications to take the deposition of the head of the Budapest Stock Exchange. I flew overnight from New York, arriving Sunday morning, and took a taxi to my hotel. As we pulled up the driveway, I saw what appeared to be dead people lying in the street, quite bloody, surrounded by 1950s ambulances. There was also a woman kneeling in a frozen posture over a wounded man. As I looked out the car window with disbelief, the driver explained to me that I was witnessing a ritual performed every year in Budapest on the anniversary of the Soviet Union's 1956 invasion of Hungary.

The next morning, I met my local counsel and traveled to the court where my deposition of the witness was to take place. Walking in the front door, I saw what appeared to be an elevator but was actually a vertical conveyor belt with rising and disappearing passenger compartments and no front door. To enter this contraption, you had to time it perfectly, stepping in at just the right moment so as not to either fall down or slam your head at the top of the open frame. The court reporter who accompanied me said she was never going to come back again.

We then appeared in the courtroom of a "junior judge" who would oversee the deposition. However, we found that we could not play by American rules, even though the deposition would be used only for the purpose of presenting the testimony in the New York courtroom where the case was pending. In courts in the United States, a deposition witness is questioned and then cross-examined as in a live trial. In Budapest, however, as in some other civil-law jurisdictions, you cannot cross-examine the witness to attack credibility and can only ask questions for clarification of the witnesses' direct testimony. After a minute of my questioning the witness on direct examination, the judge interrupted, turned to her stenographer, and then summarized in her own words the questions and the witness's answers. Notwithstanding the fact that we had flown our own stenographer from London to these proceedings, the judge told us that the only official record of the proceeding was her summary. Returning to the United States, I explained this turn of events to several of my judge friends in New York. None of them was certain whether, or how, this summary transcript could be used in a trial in their courtroom.

This experience made me think how far behind we are in integrating the operation of different legal systems to accommodate the plethora of international business transactions that are today part of our commerce. By way of contrast, a stock trader in New York and a trader in Tokyo see the same transactions on their computer screen at the same moment and communicate flawlessly as though they are sitting next to each other. Our respective judicial systems simply do not mesh in the same way.

CHAPTER 27

JUSTICE IN THE BRITISH VIRGIN ISLANDS

In the early 2000s, nine British dependent territories and formerly British (but now independent) countries in the Caribbean were the members of a treaty organization known as the Organization of Eastern Caribbean States (OECS). The OECS had a Supreme Court, which was populated by a judge from each of the nine member island countries. (No judge sat on the court in an island where he was a citizen or resident.) Appeals from a judge's decisions were taken to a four-judge Court of Appeals, presided over by the Chief Judge. Any further appeals would be taken to the Privy Council in London.

Tortola is the financial heart of the British Virgin Islands, which is one of the OECS member jurisdictions. Many international corporations are incorporated there, which is a major source of revenue because they are required to pay yearly registration fees. However, unlike the Cayman Islands, the British Virgin Islands do not have a comparable banking system, so these fees are important to the local economy. Because many corporations choose to incorporate in this jurisdiction, when there are internal legal disputes involving those corporations and their shareholders, the lawsuits are often brought there. In addition, there are actions brought in these jurisdictions for what are called *Mareva* injunctions, which afford litigants in cases or arbitrations in London the rights to seek enforcement elsewhere where assets of the defendants may be located and tied up pending a final judgment.

In 2004, the Chief Judge of the BVI Supreme Court in Tortola was concerned because complicated financial litigations were being commenced there. The court facilities, however, were not well-equipped to entertain these complex lawsuits. The judges, who were not well-paid, had no law clerks and minimal stenographic or clerical help to process these cases. Through a consultant, the Chief Judge reached out to New York court authorities to solicit advice about how to start a Commercial Court in Tortola that could better handle these cases. I was contacted and, together with Supreme Court Justice Helen Freedman and the Chief Technology Officer of the New York court system, I was invited to come to Tortola for several days of meetings with the judges, members of the Legislature, and the Governor, who is appointed by the Queen or King. We arrived and were housed in the capital of the British Virgin Islands, Road Town.

The next day, we met with the Chief Judge and were given a suggested agenda for our visit. I was dispatched to meet with the several law firms in Tortola who were the most called-upon firms to handle commercial litigation. Justice Freedman and the technology specialist were asked to meet with others in the court system. In the evening, the Chief Judge and our group were invited to meet with the Governor and his wife for dinner in the Governor's mansion. As in the British tradition, everything was ceremonial. Holding our hand-scribed invitations, we appeared at the mansion, where white-gloved, uniformed personnel opened the door of our limousine and escorted us to meet our hosts, the Governor and his wife. We had a very pleasant dinner and returned to our quarters. The next day, we met with leading members of the Legislature to discuss how commercial cases were handled in the New York court system. In the afternoon, the Chief Judge invited us on a cruise to a nearby island, where we continued our discussions and gave our impressions after having met with local lawyers.

During my meetings with commercial lawyers, I was asked if I would be interested in serving as a part-time commercial judge in Tortola. It seems that there was a latent tension between the lawyers and judges who had been trained in the British legal tradition and those who had attended local law schools. The thought was floated that an American who had no ties to either system and who had significant commercial experience might be a good candidate for a position to handle commercial cases. I thanked the lawyers for the suggestion. Over the course of several weeks, I thought about pursuing the idea. However, at the time, I had just become a senior partner in a major international law firm. At that point, I knew that my professional path would neither take me to Tortola nor keep me at a large law firm. I soon returned to my roots at a boutique litigation law firm, where, two decades later, I am still most comfortable.

CHAPTER 28

THE BROOKE ASTOR DEBACLE

Brooke Astor was perhaps the leading socialite and philanthropist in New York during the second half of the twentieth century. The Astor name became hers when she married William Vincent Astor, the son of magnate John Jacob Astor IV. The Astor name in New York traces back for generations and still is memorialized in place names such as Astor Place in Manhattan, the Astoria neighborhood in Queens, and the Waldorf-Astoria Hotel. Among other reasons, John Jacob Astor is well-known for his death on the fatal voyage of the *Titanic*. His body was found floating in the Atlantic Ocean.

It has been widely written that the relationship between Vincent Astor and his wife Brooke was problematic. Also, Vincent was very jealous of Brooke's relationship with her son, Anthony ("Tony") Marshall, born in 1924. Tony was the child of Brooke and her prior husband, John Dryden Kuser, and became the stepson of Brooke's second husband, Charles H. Marshall

III. Vincent died in 1959, leaving a fortune outright to Brooke as well as giving her control over a charitable foundation. Over several decades, Brooke was responsible for making large gifts to major New York City institutions, such as the New York Public Library and the Metropolitan Museum of Art. Celebrities and would-be celebrities tripped over themselves to be seen with her at social events attended by the elite of New York society.

Brooke lived the life of a princess, with a duplex apartment on Park Avenue and a summer home in Northeast Harbor, Maine, where she was always attended by a dozen or more servants. During Tony's adulthood, Brooke, through her political contacts, managed to arrange diplomatic ambassadorships for Tony.

Although Brooke inherited a significant fortune, the value of her investments significantly declined over time. Her son Tony stepped in to help manage her financial affairs. He was successful in restoring a significant portion of Brooke's assets and was a significant influence in her choices of charitable dispositions. However, it was reported that Brooke, both privately and publicly, was contemptuous of her son, sometimes embarrassing him in public.

Brooke turned one hundred years of age in 2003. Publicly, she appeared to be fully competent, but some in her circle began to claim that not only was Brooke suffering from dementia, but that Tony, her only son, was neglecting her and blocking expenditures for her care. As it later turned out, many of these allegations were either untrue or exaggerated. There were many in Brooke's coterie who had their own motives, good or bad, for inserting themselves into Brooke's life.

In 2006, one of Tony's sons, with whom he had a strained relationship, filed an action in New York Supreme Court to have a guardian appointed for Brooke Astor. New York law relating to guardianship is most often invoked to protect people of little means who are suffering from disability. Accordingly, the law gives judges substantial authority not only to consider guardianship of the person involved, but also the authority to look into the person's financial assets. In this court proceeding, it was ultimately agreed that Annette de la Renta would be appointed guardian of the person of Brooke, but because of the complexities of her financial circumstances, the claims concerning Tony's alleged misuse of Brooke's funds would be litigated, if at all, in an anticipated Surrogate's Court proceeding in Westchester County, where her estate would be administered upon her eventual death. Brooke Astor died the following year.

A number of prominent individuals in New York, including Annette de la Renta and Henry Kissinger, either directly or indirectly brought concerns about Tony's conduct of Brooke's financial affairs to the attention of Manhattan District Attorney Robert Morgenthau. After a long and intense investigation by that office, Tony was indicted by a New York grand jury on charges of grand larceny, receipt of stolen property, and conspiracy.

After being arraigned, Marshall was released on bail. When a charged defendant is released on bail, there are generally restrictions on his travel, and he is required to surrender any passports. On the day of his arraignment, Tony spent much of the day being processed by the District Attorney's office and the court. At the end of the court day, thoroughly exhausted and not feeling well, Tony and his wife, Charlene, returned to their apartment on the Upper East Side. He had surrendered his passport earlier that day upon his arraignment. However, after returning home, Tony and Charlene received a telephone call from an investigator at the District Attorney's office, informing them that Tony had surrendered an expired passport and that they needed to bring the current one. Charlene apologized, saying that the expired passport had been banded together with the current passport and that she would personally bring down the current one.

The next day, I had a lesson I have never forgotten about the way district attorneys operate when they perceive themselves having leverage in a high-profile case. We were notified that the District Attorney's office would be making an immediate application to the court to raise or revoke Tony's bail, based on their contention that Tony was a flight risk. Of course, that was a ridiculous assertion given Tony's age, physical condition, and lifelong roots in New York. When we arrived in court, the District Attorney's office had alerted the press, who were there in droves. The judge promptly denied the application, but the prosecutors had gotten the publicity they sought.

Tony was principally represented in the criminal matter by two experienced and highly regarded New York lawyers, Ken Warner and Fred Hafetz. In undertaking their task, they were up against not only the considerable resources of the District Attorney's office, but the tabloid press, which portrayed Tony and his wife, Charlene, as evil monsters who had preyed upon an old woman. I was called upon to provide whatever advice and assistance I could and to represent Charlene where it was prudent to have separate representation.

Among the tasks I undertook was to meet with people who had recent contact with Brooke Astor and could testify to her mental competence to make a will. These included TV legend Mike Wallace, Whoopi Goldberg, and others. Another person I met with at my office was David Richenthal, who was then producing a Broadway revival of Arthur Miller's *Death of a Salesman*. Ironically, Miller's granddaughter (the daughter of my old friend

Bobby Miller) was interning for me at the time, and I called her to introduce her to Richenthal.

While much has been written about the trial and the ultimate conviction of Tony on a number of counts, there are a number of features about this sad prosecution that made me aware of grossly unfair aspects of the criminal justice system—of which the public only gets occasional glimpses. At the time of the criminal trial, Tony was in poor health at age eighty-five and, like any defendant, was required to be in court every day. Each time he would appear at the courthouse, cameras would be put in his face as reporters tripped over themselves both to photograph him and bait him with questions. During breaks in the proceedings, he had no privacy as he made his way to the men's room. On one occasion, I was sitting with Charlene in the gallery when a person in the row behind us was breathing on Charlene's neck, stalking her. She gasped and the proceeding was interrupted. After the trial day, the press would always be sure to send somebody to confront the couple when, exhausted after a long day, they would return to their apartment on East 79th Street.

One of the counts of the indictment for which Tony was convicted required the judge to impose a sentence of at least one year's imprisonment. Following the trial, Tony took an appeal to the Appellate Division of the Supreme Court. However, Tony was to be incarcerated before the date when his appeal would be heard. A convicted defendant has a right in New York to ask any single judge of the Appellate Division to issue a stay of a prison sentence while his appeal is pending. Ken Warner and I appeared *ex parte* in chambers before Justice Helen Freedman of the Appellate Division and argued for a stay. She granted the application. However, the very next morning, a panel of her appellate court was assembled remotely and reversed the stay. Tony had to report to jail.

In anticipation of this possible result, the lawyers for Tony had discussed with the District Attorney's office and other officials the fact that Tony was quite ill. They were assured that Tony's medical needs would be adequately cared for when he was confined. On a Friday afternoon, Tony surrendered and was driven to Rikers Island in New York City's East River. It is a notorious facility where people are confined either before trial, if not released, or for short sentences after conviction. There have been horror stories about the facility and investigations that have produced reports of beatings and other crimes at the facility.

On Monday, I visited Tony at Rikers Island. I had been there only once before, when I visited the flamboyant Abe Hirschfeld, who at his second trial was convicted of planning to kill his partner in various real-estate partnerships, Stanley Stahl. I had previously represented Hirschfeld in a civil litigation between him and the Stahl estate until I had to withdraw as counsel when Hirschfeld threatened the trial judge. Hirschfeld not only was a significant player in New York real estate, but he had bought and sold the *New York Post* and had publicly offered to pay $1 million to Bill Clinton to allow him to settle the harassment lawsuit brought by Paula Jones.

My trip to Rikers Island to visit Tony Marshall brought back memories of my visit to see Hirschfeld some years before. For someone who doesn't work or visit there regularly, it is an unsettling experience. Entering the complex from Queens, you see a causeway over the water guarded by law enforcement with semi-automatic rifles. There is a crude reception area where family members visiting the inmates during limited hours were in a crowded line to await their clearance. As a lawyer, I checked in at a separate counter where nobody else was waiting, displayed my credentials, and said I was visiting Hirschfeld. What seemed like my special treatment was only available because court decisions had required authorities to give lawyers liberal access to their incarcerated clients. After getting clearance, I drove my vehicle over the deserted causeway to the island, where there was a designated parking lot. It was a hot summer day, and I waited in the sun for the arrival of a shuttle bus—an old school bus that had no air-conditioning and rattled loudly. I disembarked at the entrance to the complex of cells and because I had a lawyer pass, much to my surprise, I was not screened or searched. Passing through two electronically controlled doors, I was escorted into a small room in hospital quarters where Hirschfeld was isolated. There were two chairs for Hirschfeld and me to speak. A third chair was occupied by a corrections officer who sat about ten feet away to monitor us. After Hirschfeld and I had spoken for about twenty minutes, the officer appeared to be dozing off.

Coming back to my present senses, as I made my way to visit Tony Marshall, I was again escorted to a small room where he waited for me. I was startled at what I saw. This once-decorated veteran of Iwo Jima was dirty and disheveled without any fresh clothing. He appeared quite confused. He also had bruises. I later learned that he had been beaten and at one point, he had dropped some food he had been given, and because he had difficulty picking it up, only the kindness of another inmate allowed his food to be retrieved. I reflected with a degree of anger on the hollow assurances that had been given about the good care the corrections system would provide him at Rikers. Tony was later transferred to a facility about forty miles away in Fishkill, New York, where Charlene rented a room so she could visit Tony every day. At some point, the authorities realized that Tony's medical needs were beyond their capacity to provide for. I am sure that they did not want to be embarrassed in this high-profile case should Tony die on their watch. He was released early due to his medical circumstances.

During this ordeal, I learned how cruel the tabloid press could be. All through the pretrial and trial proceedings, the press would follow the couple and print pictures of Charlene, referring to her as "Miss Piggy." I paid one or two visits to Tony and Charlene at their Upper East Side home in the weeks that followed Tony's release. Charlene was tending to his care twenty-four hours a day, while Tony seemed completely disoriented and anxious. It was not long before he passed away.

I often reflected on how decent this couple was, treating everybody around them with courtesy and respect. When one visited them at their apartment, Tony was always dressed during the day in a blazer and tie. I spent time with them on two or three occasions in their summer home in Northeast Harbor, Maine, which Tony had inherited from his mother, Brooke Astor. On one occasion there, Charlene brought me to the summer home of Martha Stewart, where her staff invited us in to view the lovely home. I made a mental note how the furniture was fully covered to protect it from sunlight. It occurred to me that even the wealthy and famous, in their privacy, have the same concerns that others have.

One other moment remains in my memory. One afternoon, I brought my son Daniel, then about sixteen years old, to visit Tony and Charlene in their Manhattan apartment. Tony reached into a drawer and pulled out an antique pocket watch and showed it to my son. He explained that this was the watch found on John Jacob Astor as he floated on the ocean after the *Titanic* sank.

CHAPTER 29

THE FALL OF A GIANT: THE DEMISE OF DEWEY LEBOEUF

In early 2012, the national press began to report that one of the nation's most prominent law firms, Dewey & LeBoeuf LLP, was in financial difficulty following a number of partner departures. Management initially issued statements denying these stories, but several weeks later, the law firm filed for bankruptcy. Reading the story, I recalled memories of an earlier such financial collapse in 1987, when the law firm of Finley Kumble had failed, a spectacle in which I represented one of the prominent partners. The Finley Kumble firm had achieved prominence in large part because it brought on as partners former politicians, guaranteeing them substantial compensation. Included among them were former Nevada Senator Paul Laxalt, former New York Governor Hugh Carey, and former New York City Mayor Robert Wagner. What Finley Kumble's management had not made known to most of the partners was that the law firm had been borrowing money heavily to pay the bloated compensation of these prominent partners.

For those not familiar with bankruptcy procedures, it is common for the Bankruptcy Court, at the request of creditors, to appoint a trustee to oversee the debtor's business affairs. One of the trustee's primary responsibilities is to attempt to enlarge the debtor's estate by bringing claims against persons or entities that either owe money to the debtor or were favored with payments from the debtor. Whatever is recovered by the trustee is paid out in a prescribed order that generally favors secured creditors (such as banks that have lent money to the debtor in return for collateral) over unsecured creditors.

One of the important tools available to the trustee is to try to "claw back" money from partners in a law firm who were distributed profits if the firm was insolvent at the time of those distributions. In the Finley Kumble case, the trustee, a senior partner in the Milbank Tweed law firm, devised a proposed plan to settle claims against the partners by dividing the partners into two groups: those in the management group who were highly compensated, and those less highly compensated partners who essentially had been in the dark about the law firm's financial affairs. This latter group came to be known in some circles as "mushrooms," because they were "in the dark and fed shit." It was also proposed that one lawyer represent the members of each of the two groups so that legal costs to the partners would be reduced. The trustee's plan was to propose higher percentages of clawback of their compensation for those in the management group as compared to the "mushrooms."

The Finley Kumble partner I represented did not want to be included in either group. He had had the misfortune of being elected to the firm's management committee just weeks before the collapse and did not believe he should be included in the management group; and the trustee would not be willing to treat him as a member of the mushrooms. What followed was a complex negotiation between the trustee and lawyers for the parties, including me, that resulted in a settlement that potentially saved partners much greater liabilities.

When Dewey LeBoeuf cratered, I knew that it would not be long before I would get a phone call. That distinguished law firm represented a combination of two old and prestigious firms: Dewey Ballantine and LeBoeuf, Lamb, Greene & MacRae. The Dewey in the firm name was none other than former New York District Attorney Thomas E. Dewey, who later became Governor of New York and then ran unsuccessfully for President against Harry S. Truman in 1948. The LeBoeuf firm had represented major national corporations, including International Telephone & Telegraph (ITT).

When my phone rang, I was asked to represent a group of fifty-seven partners in the Dewey LeBoeuf bankruptcy. There, as in the Finley Kumble bankruptcy, the trustee proposed to sue the partners to claw back several years of their compensation, claiming that during those years the firm had actually been insolvent. The trustee hired a consulting firm headed by former New York City Comptroller Harrison Goldin to come up with a settlement plan for proposed clawback settlement amounts that would be substantial, but less than the trustee might be able to achieve in suing the partners on behalf of the law firm's estate.

The first challenge I faced was how to effectively represent fifty-seven individual partners located around the country, many of whom were anxious and feared for their own financial survival. So I came up with a plan to make the representation manageable.

Because I could not feasibly consult with fifty-seven different clients with multiple, differing views on strategy, we established a committee of four partners who would, by agreement of the others, make all strategic decisions in consultation with me. In addition, since it would be impractical to send bills to fifty-seven clients and collect from each, a fund was established from which legal bills could be paid, with the committee responsible for having the individual partners contribute to the fund. If the fund could no longer be maintained to keep up with our legal work, we would have the right to withdraw as counsel. By this arrangement, no partner would be individually liable to pay legal fees to our firm.

During the course of litigation, I do not normally reach out to the press. In this circumstance, however, I felt it was necessary to do so. The consulting firm retained by the trustee came up with a proposed settlement plan for clawback of partners' income for the past several years. This would not only be a severe hardship for many partners, but in some cases could result in personal bankruptcy. This result would be particularly cruel, since most of the partners were completely unaware of the details of the firm's finances, which had been closely managed by a few firm leaders. It was my decision to push back on these demands. I told the press that we would ask the court to come down hard on the firm leaders who had benefitted most from any financial manipulation. The goal in going public was twofold: to give some reassurance to my clients, and to send a message to firm management that we would fight them. If successful, the result would be that the highly compensated members of firm management would agree to pay a larger share of the aggregate amount being demanded by the trustee. As often happens in the resolution of disputes, the result of the compromise was that the highly compensated partners agreed to increase their contribution while some of the creditors agreed to accept a reduced payment. Part of this agreement relieved recently retired partners, who had been inactive during the relevant time period but received payouts for their earlier work, from any liability to contribute to the clawback.

As I learned over time, most of the partners moved on from this debacle to continue their successful professional lives. But this case served as a warning to much of the legal community to manage their financial affairs more conservatively and more openly. This was a lesson that had apparently not taken hold in the earlier Finley Kumble case.

CHAPTER 30

THE SHERIFF OF WALL STREET AND THE CHAIRMAN

Richard Grasso is a Horatio Alger story writ large. The son of a working-class family, he may have been the least probable person ever to end up as Chairman of the New York Stock Exchange.

Grasso, born in Queens, went to work as a clerk at the stock exchange as his first job after leaving the army. Over the ensuing years, Grasso worked his way up the ranks until he became the exchange's President and Chief Executive Officer in the early 1990s. Grasso was by all accounts a successful CEO, helping to keep the New York Stock Exchange as the most prestigious in the country. His compensation for these services rose over time until by 2003 it was reported to be in excess of $180 million. Some officials including the head of the SEC criticized this compensation package as excessive, and in September 2003, the NYSE Board voted 13–7 to ask Grasso to resign, which he did.

In 2004, the Attorney General of the State of New York, Eliot Spitzer, sued Grasso in Manhattan, alleging that Grasso's compensation was grossly excessive and seeking a court order requiring him to return much of it. The Attorney General's lawsuit was assigned to Supreme Court Justice Charles E. Ramos, an experienced judge. It was clear that he took a strong personal interest in this high-profile litigation.

Grasso's personal attorney was Brendan Sullivan of the Wahington, D.C., law firm of Williams & Connolly. Although he handled many important ligations over the years, Sullivan was particularly known to the public for his aggressive defense before Congress of Colonel Oliver North during the Iran-Contra hearings. He is remembered for his exclamation, "I am not a potted plant." In the Grasso litigation, he was joined by his brilliant colleague, Gerson Zweifach, also of Williams & Connolly, and a team of able lawyers from that firm. Since the litigation was in New York, the team reached out to me to act as their cocounsel for Grasso.

One day, we received a somewhat mysterious phone call from the Attorney General's office requesting us to join them in a private conference with the court and counsel. We appeared in the anteroom of Justice Ramos's courtroom with the lawyers for the Attorney General and the New York Stock Exchange, whose bidding the Attorney General was doing. Counsel from the Attorney General's office told the judge that among the documents located in the Stock Exchange's files was a letter written by or on behalf of Justice Ramos asking that he be considered for a seat on the Board of the New York Stock Exchange upon his anticipated retirement. The letter had arrived when Grasso was still Chairman of the Exchange, but it was never answered. Justice Ramos disclaimed any recollection of it. The obvious issue in the air was whether or not this circumstance should prompt a request for Justice Ramos to recuse himself, but it was not pursued by us.

Some time later, yet another letter appeared. The content of this letter was closely related to the very issues being litigated in the Grasso lawsuit. A "headhunter" (the common name for a recruiter) had written to the Stock Exchange again promoting Ramos as a candidate for director, expressly noting that Ramos had been the judge in another case involving allegedly high compensation at a not-for-profit institution, Adelphi University. The suggestion was that a judge such as Ramos would be particularly empathetic to claims of excessive compensation—the very issue in the Grasso case. Again, no request was made for Justice Ramos to recuse himself.

One day, Justice Ramos demanded to have settlement discussions separately with Attorney General Eliot Spitzer and then with Richard Grasso. After much discussion, the Grasso team agreed and Sullivan, Zweifach, and Grasso met me at my office, from which we traveled to the courthouse. We entered the large empty courtroom, where Justice Ramos was waiting in the anteroom. I asked Grasso and the attorneys on our team to wait outside while I went in to see Justice Ramos. Since I knew him well, and our relationship was cordial, I told the justice that I would be pleased to bring in Mr. Grasso, but on one condition: if Justice Ramos were to delve into the merits of the case as part of his efforts to promote settlement, he would recuse himself from the litigation if no settlement was reached. I recall that he agreed. I brought in Mr. Grasso and the other attorneys on our team. Judge Ramos began by making some very flattering remarks about Grasso's remarkable career but then raised the temperature, beginning to allude to certain facts in the case that he suggested should persuade Grasso to settle. Grasso held his ground and the conference adjourned without any movement towards settlement.

Following this meeting, we made a motion asking Judge Ramos to recuse himself based on the fact that, in my view, he had discussed and expressed a view on the merits of the case. He denied the motion, stating in an affidavit that he had not done so. Judge Ramos's refusal to recuse himself on the basis of the two letters and the settlement conference was challenged in the Appellate Division, which held that he had acted within his discretion. After much litigation, Grasso prevailed in a series of rulings culminating in a unanimous decision by the New York Court of Appeals in 2008, written by Chief Judge Judith S. Kaye, which held that Grasso's compensation, while high, did not violate the New York Not-for-Profit Corporation Law and was not subject to challenge by the Attorney General.

Dick Grasso has often told me over the years that he was grateful for my efforts. But I am the one who is most grateful for having had the opportunity to play a role in his having prevailed in this hard-knuckled, drawn-out fight.

CHAPTER 31

SENATOR EUGENE MCCARTHY: A BLAST FROM THE PAST

Elsewhere in this book, I have recounted some of the turbulent events of 1968, including the Martin Luther King, Jr., and Robert F. Kennedy assassinations. In the spring, President Lyndon Johnson unexpectedly announced that he would not run for reelection in the fall. All of these events were precursors to the presidential election of 1968 and the fierce contest among Democratic contenders for the nomination to oppose Richard Nixon. Among those contenders was Senator Eugene McCarthy, representing the liberal wing of the party, against Senator Hubert Humphrey, then the incumbent Vice President under Lyndon Johnson. Humphrey was closely tied to President Johnson's deeply unpopular Vietnam War policy. The internal struggle reached a head in the infamous Democratic National Convention and the unrest in Chicago that led to allegations of police brutality and the prosecution of the Chicago Seven. When the literal and figurative bloodshed ended, Humphrey won the nomination. He went on to lose the election to Nixon in November 1968.

But McCarthy was not finished. Twenty-four years later, in 1992, he sought, but was denied, the opportunity to participate in the televised presidential candidate debates among Democrats. In 1995, McCarthy brought a lawsuit in federal court in New York, alleging that the television networks and the Democratic National Committee and Ron Brown, its Chairman, had wrongfully excluded him from the televised debates. At the time he brought his lawsuit, Brown had moved on and was serving as President Bill Clinton's Secretary of Commerce. The General Counsel of the Democratic National Committee called me and asked if I would represent Secretary Brown in the lawsuit. I said I would.

But there was a problem. It turns out that my law firm, Stein, Zauderer, Ellenhorn, Frischer & Sharp, was participating with the law firm of Cravath, Swaine & Moore in representing the City of New York in a *pro bono* lawsuit against the U.S. Department of Commerce, of which Brown was currently the cabinet Secretary. That lawsuit alleged that the Commerce Department, which administers the national census every ten years, had wrongfully omitted many New York residents from the census count. In this peculiar situation, it appeared that I might have a conflict in representing Brown in McCarthy's lawsuit. However, the Justice Department got involved and issued a legal opinion that paved the way for me to represent Secretary Brown.

McCarthy's lawsuit did not get traction with Federal Judge John Martin, who dismissed the case in a decision affirmed by the Second Circuit Court of Appeals. Tragically, however,

Brown later died in a plane crash. At one of the court hearings, I appeared and joined a phalanx of lawyers representing the defendant television networks. Present was McCarthy himself, who knew I was part of the opposition. He approached me in the courtroom and handed me, with a smile, a signed copy of his recent book. If nothing else, he was a perfect gentleman.

CHAPTER 32

BROADWAY COMES TO COURT

Most people associate Broadway with high-end theater, entertainment, and the excitement of New York City. However, there is another side of Broadway that is generally less visible to the public: litigation over money.

In 1983, the Rogers & Hart musical *On Your Toes* was revived on Broadway to great success. That year, the musical won the Tony Award for Best Revival. Yet, there was a darker side masked by the attendant celebration.

The producers of the show included Roger L. Stevens, who was the director of the John F. Kennedy Center for the Performing Arts in Washington. As was common, the production first opened out-of-town, in Seattle, as a test run of its likely success if brought to New York City. At the time, Andre Pastoria, a young man from West Virginia who had been an associate producer of the musical *On the Twentieth Century* a year earlier, sought to put together a group of investors to help bring the production of *On*

Your Toes to New York. The group was persuaded to invest and have Mr. Pastoria act as a co-producer with Stevens.

Subsequently, the group filed a lawsuit against Pastoria, as well as Stevens, claiming that, contrary to what they had been told the funds would be used for, they were instead applied to bail the production out from significant debt linked to the earlier Seattle production. Pastoria retained me to defend him from the suit brought against him in New York Supreme Court by his own investors. Responding on behalf of Pastoria, we denied the lawsuit's allegations insofar as they pertained to him and asserted that it was only Stevens who knew the actual facts of the use of the investors' funds.

The lawsuit provided me with a number of new perspectives on the world of Broadway. My client enthusiastically invited me to see the show on a number of occasions. I recall that one night after the show, we went out for late dinks with many in the cast, including Natalia Makarova, the world-famous ballerina, who won a separate Tony Award for Best Actress in a musical; Kitty Carlisle Hart, the widow of Moss Hart and then the director of the New York State Council on the Arts; and actress Dina Merrill, the wife of actor Cliff Robertson. Merrill's father was E.F. Hutton and her mother was Marjorie Merriweather Post, once known as the wealthiest woman in the United States (she owned many mansions, including Mar-a-Lago in Palm Beach, Florida). What struck me in my interaction with the cast was their humanity and their love for their craft. Money seemed to be the last thing on their minds.

My job as a lawyer took me into a real world far from the stage life on Broadway. On a cold winter day, I traveled with my client to the Kennedy Center to conduct a court-ordered inspection of the books and records maintained there. Entering the large auditorium, I was struck by its vast emptiness as we scanned the scene. We then proceeded to some small offices outside the public areas, where we inspected business records that were no different from those associated with any business.

The lawsuit was eventually settled, but my experience reenforced my long-held belief that the heart of a trial lawyer's skill is an understanding of human behavior, a knowledge of the law, and the mastery of the litigation process. A lawyer who possesses those attributes is one who can effectively represent clients no matter what the particular subject matter of the dispute.

CHAPTER 33

UNIVERSITIES ARE NOT JUST ABOUT LEARNING

Many are unaware of the variety of litigations that universities find themselves enmeshed in. These run the gamut from civil-rights suits, to patent and technology suits, to claims to undersea treasure, to real-estate disputes, to insider trading investigations. I have been involved in many of these. But one that was particularly interesting was my retention by Columbia University to defend it in a defamation lawsuit.

Over many decades, the university maintained a residential building that was made available primarily to faculty members and their families. In the building was a school for young children, who were frequently taken to the roof playground above the tenth floor. Hostility developed between the teachers and a tenth-floor resident, which ended up in screaming matches when the resident approached the teachers to complain.

As a result, the school hired a security guard to sit in the lobby of the building. According to a lawsuit filed by the tenth-floor resident, one day another longtime resident of the building, U.S. District Judge Richard Owen, came down to the lobby and, seeing the security guard, asked him what he was doing there. The guard responded, "I am here to protect the children from the child molester on the tenth floor." According to the tenth-floor resident, the plaintiff in the lawsuit, this statement was defamatory—and particularly so because he was gay. In his lawsuit, plaintiff named as defendants the school, the security guard service, and Columbia University.

Beginning my representation, I called Judge Owen in his chambers to introduce myself and asked him whether what the plaintiff alleged about his seeing the security guard was accurate. He said that it was, and he invited me to come meet with him at his chambers in the courthouse. It was clear that he would be a witness in this case.

When I arrived at the judge's chambers, he politely invited me to come in to discuss the matter. He mentioned to me that his wife was friendly with the plaintiff but did not say much more about the events at issue. I left his chambers after telling him I would have to take his deposition. The judge said he understood that.

Some months later, the lawyers assembled with a court reporter to take the judge's testimony in his chambers. I questioned Judge Owen in some detail, asking him what he knew about any confrontations between the plaintiff and the teachers. He said that he knew a lot about it. I asked him, "How?" He then told me for the first time that he had a tape recording of such a confrontation. I asked him if he had it available. He said, "Yes. Would you like me to play it for you?" As many people know, Judge Owen was an opera buff and something of a composer. Accordingly, he had a professional sound system in his chambers.

He proceeded to play a tape that reflected loud screaming, which he testified was a typical confrontation between the plaintiff and teachers on the roof of his building.

Judge Owen confirmed under oath the statement he heard about the "child molester on the tenth floor." I asked him, "Was anyone else present?" He said "No." I then asked him, "When you heard that, did you believe the characterization of the plaintiff as a child molester was true?" The judge replied, "Absolutely not." After finishing the deposition, I suggested to the judge that he counsel the plaintiff that there could be no damages awarded in this case because the plaintiff's reputation could not possibly have been harmed, since the judge was the only person who heard the statement at issue, and, by his own testimony, he did not believe it.

In my experience, while judges can be very astute in evaluating the people and circumstances presented to them in their judicial role, they sometimes have no more clarity or objectivity than anyone else in assessing events in which they are involved personally. I thought this unusual lawsuit and the judge's role in it provided a good illustration of this point.

CHAPTER 34

ALL IN THE FAMILY

Many of the immigrants who landed in New York City in the late nineteenth and early twentieth centuries were virtually destitute on arrival. Yet in this land of relative opportunity, they found creative ways to eke out a living. Some began with pushcarts on the Lower East Side of Manhattan. Others pooled their meager funds and purchased walk-up flats. And some began manufacturing clothing, leading eventually to the development of the garment industry in Manhattan. It was common for siblings of the same generation to start small businesses. In many cases, they paid little attention to the paperwork formalities that we associate with business corporations or partnerships. The profits were divided up informally, often in accordance with individual needs.

Over the decades, like saplings that grow into strong trees, many of these ventures took root and provided wealth for the entrepreneurs and their offspring. I have encountered many times in my legal career families whose grandparents purchased a building or two and who now own collectively dozens of buildings that generate millions of dollars each year. But the good fortune of these families often generates bitter legal battles. The founding generations would be saddened to witness the family discord that often develops.

One dispute that came to me that illustrates this dynamic involved an oil company in New York founded by four brothers in the 1950s. They had the good sense to sign on to a basic shareholders' agreement that defined their rights. Over the decades, as the business grew, interests diverged. One branch of the family, the one running the business, voted themselves substantial compensation, while family members not drawing salaries enjoyed only modest benefits through meager shareholder dividends. This pattern is a very common generator of disputes as the generations diverge. But there was another irritant. The shareholders' agreement that the four founding brothers had created provided that if one of them died, their stock could only pass to a male child of his family; in the absence of a male child, the brother's interest would be purchased by the other surviving brothers. One of the brothers had only daughters. Their father was ill and became less active in the business. When he died, the other brothers put together a plan to take the business public and profit handsomely—much to the disadvantage of the two daughters.

As those controlling the company were organizing a "road show" to tout the "going public" transaction, the two daughters retained me to try to stop it. On a Friday morning, we filed a lawsuit in Supreme Court seeking an injunction against the transaction, arguing among other things that the gender restriction in the shareholders' agreement was illegal. Without any opposing lawyers present, we obtained from the judge an *ex parte* restraining order that stopped the transaction in its tracks. An order to show cause signed by the judge set the matter down for a prompt hearing the following Tuesday. At the appointed time, the opposing lawyer appeared and urged the court to lift the restraining order, complaining that it was killing the transaction. The judge declined to do so and set the matter down for further briefing, which meant that it wouldn't be decided for weeks or more. As a result, Wall Street lost interest and, sure enough the "going public" transaction died.

Lawyers who litigate in New York know that the longstanding practice in New York of courts granting *ex parte* temporary restraining orders, without giving the other side any advance notice, virtually came to a stop several years later, when the court rules were amended to require that adversaries be alerted to those applications (with certain specified exceptions) to afford them the opportunity to be present. In this instance, ultimately a settlement was reached that resulted in fair compensation to the daughters for the sale of their stock.

A second example of diverging interests over the generations is the case of the M. Fine & Sons Manufacturing Company. Founded in 1890 by Morris Fine, the company grew to become a major manufacturer of men's work clothes. One of its top-selling brands was Dakota Jeans. One hundred years later, the business was run by two branches of the Fine family: one in New York and the other in Louisville, Kentucky. As is so often the case, tension arose between those in active management of the business and other descendants of Morris Fine who were dissatisfied with their shareholder dividends. Litigation ensued, and after considerable time and expense, the matter settled, with the inactive family members having their interests brought out. I was representing the selling shareholders and expected the buy-out transaction to close shortly. But once again there was a problem.

On a hot weekend day, I was aboard *Different Drummer*, docked at the Mystic Seaport Museum in Mystic, Connecticut. I received an urgent call on ship-to-shore radio (this was in the infancy of cellphones) to call the lawyers representing other selling parties. I learned that there was litigation in South Dakota initiated by a man who claimed to have trademark rights to the Dakota brand. Unless this could be resolved, the whole deal would be killed. There was only one phone booth on the docks, and I spent two hours on and off in the sweltering booth while other visitors complained that I was hogging it. I was given a phone number and was asked to make contact with the man in South Dakota who supposedly had rights to the Dakota trademark. Meanwhile, my infant son, Daniel, and his babysitter remained on board *Different Drummer*.

Sure enough, I reached this person. He was a very proud man who said he was deeply offended by the company's refusal to recognize his Dakota trademark. He said he would consider resolving the matter only if I personally came to South Dakota to meet him at a certain place. I did as he asked and the next day I flew to Sioux Falls and met him on the rocks of a scenic hill outside of the city. There we spoke for about an hour. By the end, we had laid the groundwork for a settlement. It was obvious that the key to a settlement was less about the financial terms than the fact that he wanted to be shown respect. Having accorded him what he needed, we settled the matter, and the Fine family problem was resolved.

CHAPTER 35

NEW YORK BECOMES A LEADER IN GLOBAL COMMERCIAL LITIGATION

When I started my career, the common belief among lawyers in major New York City law firms was that the New York State courts were no place to commence a complex commercial litigation. Most cases were commenced in the federal court in Manhattan. However, the federal courts have limited subject matter jurisdiction, so that sometimes there was no choice but to commence a case in state Supreme Court.

Although there were always some very capable jurists among the state court judiciary, the court system was not well equipped to handle the procedural complexities of these cases, and judges had minimal staff to assist in the necessary legal research and writing involved. Personal injury and medical malpractice cases constituted the bulk of the court docket, which are procedurally simpler than commercial cases; the latter generally require significant oversight during the pretrial phase by the judge who will ultimately be trying the case. Until January 1, 1986, cases were not assigned to a single judge for all purposes; each pretrial motion would be decided by a different judge, with each judge having no real familiarity with the prior history of the case.

In 1995, Chief Judge Judith S. Kaye, who had been a commercial litigator in private practice, determined to make the New York State courts a more hospitable forum for commercial cases. She assembled a task force, on which I served as a member, to create the Commercial Division within the court system to entertain these complex cases. Since that time, judges with special experience and interest in commercial matters have been appointed to that Division, and the Commercial Division Advisory Council, on which I serve, continuously proposes new rules and procedures to ensure that the Division has adequate resources to provide a climate hospitable to commercial interests. Successive governors and chief judges have, over the past several decades, deemed it in the state's best interests to encourage businesses to consider New York State courts as the forum of choice for resolution of commercial disputes. One high profile case in which I have been involved illustrates how successful this court initiative has been.

Asked by well-known lawyer Bill Reid of Reid Collins & Tsai LLP to join him as co-counsel in *In re Renren Inc. Derivative Litigation*, I recognized that the case presented unique legal and evidentiary challenges for both the parties and the court. It involved a complex intersection of international corporate structure, New York securities law, fiduciary duty, jurisdictional reach, and derivative standing under Cayman Islands law. From the outset, I also knew that, by partnering with Bill and his talented team, we had assembled a group of advocates capable of confronting those challenges directly and achieving success.

Renren, once hailed as the "Facebook of China," went public on the New York Stock Exchange in 2011, raising nearly $800 million from investors worldwide. But as its social-networking business declined, Renren's controlling insiders, led by founder and CEO Joseph Chen, sought a way to extract the company's valuable investment portfolio, including a major stake in the California fintech company SoFi.

The China-based insiders labeled it a "spin-off." In reality, it was what New York Supreme Court Justice Andrew Borrok later called an effort to "loot[] Renren and its shareholders of its most valuable assets." The assets were transferred to a private Cayman entity controlled by Chen and his allies, leaving minority shareholders with little more than an empty shell.

When the case reached Justice Borrok in 2019, shortly after his appointment to the Commercial Division, which was designed to handle precisely such complex transnational disputes, the central question was whether New York had jurisdiction over a corporate dispute involving a Cayman-incorporated, China-based issuer. In a 2020 decision denying the defendants' motions to dismiss, Justice Borrok answered yes. He held that the misconduct was orchestrated through New York's financial markets, that Renren had intentionally chosen this forum when it raised capital from U.S. investors, and that New York's courts therefore had both jurisdiction and a duty to act. The ruling marked a turning point, establishing that the Commercial Division of New York's Supreme Court would not allow global fiduciaries to misuse New York's markets as a shield for misconduct.

By 2021, evidence revealed that the defendants were liquidating the assets at issue, particularly Renren's SoFi shares, and transferring proceeds through offshore accounts. Fearing that the assets would be dissipated beyond reach, we sought emergency relief. Justice Borrok responded with one of the most significant equitable rulings in recent Commercial Division history: a pre-judgment order of attachment under CPLR 6201(3).

The order froze hundreds of millions of dollars in proceeds linked to the self-dealing transactions, required affidavits identifying the beneficial owners and the location of funds, and clarified that those proceeds must remain available to satisfy any eventual judgment. Such pre-judgment attachments are not common, and Justice Borrok's ruling demonstrated his willingness to use the New York court's full equitable power to prevent a judgment from becoming meaningless. His decision sent a clear signal that sophisticated foreign actors could not use complex offshore structures to escape accountability once they accessed New York's markets.

The defendants appealed, but the Appellate Division, First Department, unanimously upheld Justice Borrok's rulings on both jurisdiction and attachment, confirming that New York courts have authority over foreign insiders who exploit its capital markets for self-dealing.

The resulting settlement was historic. On June 9, 2022, Justice Borrok approved a direct-pay cash settlement of at least $300 million for minority shareholders, one of the largest cash recoveries ever approved in a New York derivative action. Subsequent proceedings refined the structure and distribution of those funds, and the First Department again upheld Justice Borrok's reasoning, ruling that any recovery must go to the shareholders who actually experienced the injury and that counsel fees should remain proportional to the benefit provided.

By the time the appellate process concluded and the settlement was implemented, *Renren* had produced a series of decisions that collectively broke new ground: asserting jurisdiction over global fiduciary fraud, using attachment as a protective remedy, and ensuring fair distribution in complex derivative recoveries. The case redefined New York's role as a protector of market integrity in an interconnected financial world. It also reflects the enduring vision of Chief Judge Kaye, and her successor Chief Judge Jonathan Lippman, behind the creation of the Commercial Division. That innovation transformed New York from a regional commercial center into a global judicial forum capable of resolving disputes at the highest levels of international finance and commerce.

CHAPTER 36

COMMUTING TO LONDON—AND ANOTHER SMOKING GUN

In the spring of 1992, I was sitting at my desk when a call came from someone named David Hammond. He was calling at 9:00 p.m. from his car in London and said that my name had been given to him by a lawyer I knew. Hammond introduced himself as the Vice Chairman of ADT, an international security-alarm company, and said that they had a legal problem. Through an offshore subsidiary, Itoba, Ltd., located in the Isle of Jersey, the company had purchased shares on the London exchange of a foreign company that had a competing subsidiary in the security alarm business. That company had just released extremely troubling details of its business that sent the price of its stock plummeting. Hammond wanted to bring a lawsuit in the United States and asked if I would be interested. I said that I was, and he said, "Good. I'll have someone at your office in the morning."

I wondered how someone might find a flight that late from London to New York—but didn't realize at the time that people at this corporate level did not fly commercial.

Sure enough, Nick Wells appeared at my office the next morning to discuss the matter, and in short order we were retained. After we had the opportunity to review relevant documents, I saw asked to come to London to discuss the matter. This invitation led to the first of many trips to London. About a month later, based on information we had obtained, we filed a securities-fraud lawsuit in the United States District Court for the District of Connecticut. We chose that venue because a key board member, a wealthy investor, resided there. Our complaint alleged violations of the securities laws based on the company's failure to reveal highly significant business problems that our investigation led us to believe were known to the company and not disclosed to the public.

Predictably, the company gathered its legal forces and filed a motion to dismiss the complaint on the ground that the transaction—ADT's subsidiary's purchase of shares on the London exchange—was not sufficiently tied to the United States to give the U.S. court what is known as subject-matter jurisdiction, because it was essentially a foreign transaction that did not come within the reach of the U.S. securities laws. We opposed the motion and were eager to go forward with discovery to peek behind the curtain to prove our case. The Connecticut District Judge, Warren W. Eginton, referred the matter to Magistrate Judge Joan G. Margolis, who declined to let us go forward with full discovery and limited discovery to facts relevant only to subject-matter jurisdiction.

This delayed the progress of the case for over two years. Limited depositions were taken and further submissions were made to the Magistrate Judge. She ultimately recommended that Itoba's case be dismissed for lack of subject-matter jurisdiction. We appealed that recommendation to Judge Eginton, who swiftly adopted it before we even had a chance to submit our final set of papers to him. We took an appeal to the United States Court of Appeals for the Second Circuit. Finally, after briefing and oral argument, on May 15, 1995, that Appellate Court reversed the District Court, reinstating the case and finding that the Court had jurisdiction based in part on the company's filings with the SEC and issuance of ADRs (American depositary receipts) in the United States, all of which the Court found had been overlooked by Magistrate Judge Margolis and the District Court. In particular, the Court of Appeals decision was critical of the Magistrate Judge's legal analysis. We are all familiar with the axiom that justice delayed is justice denied. In this case, during the long period of time it took to have the case reinstated, the company had become virtually worthless, and the only defendant within our grasp was the board member resident in Connecticut.

Given the frequency with which I had to travel to London during the course of discovery and meetings with the client, I developed a routine that would allow me to conduct business there without being exhausted when I arrived. I would typically fly to London on Sunday morning, arriving in the evening. At first, to save travel time, I would book the Concorde, the iconic aircraft that seemed to be more a symbol of prestige for travelers than a practical necessity. The seats, two abreast, were not more comfortable than the typical business-class seats that do not fully recline. Given the somewhat cramped quarters, the food preparation seemed not up to the level provided in business or first class. The main attraction, apart from the speed with which one traveled to the destination, was a screen in the cabin that displayed the velocity of the airplane, which ultimately reached about 1,300 miles per hour, or double the speed of sound. Passengers who traveled on this plane would sometimes tell others about the jolt of acceleration they experienced when the pilot, after leaving the restricted space over land, would kick in the plane's afterburners. In reality, the barely perceptible jolt was not much more than one would experience when stepping down on the accelerator of a Chevrolet Nova. The plane would arrive in London mid-afternoon rather than early evening, not a meaningful difference on a Sunday. Moreover, the in-cabin experience even in business class on conventional airplanes was superior to that of the Concorde. One interesting feature of the Concorde that stands out was the window in the mid-plane galley area. You could place your hand on the window and feel the significant heat generated by friction as the plane traveled supersonically at nearly sixty thousand feet.

Based on a recommendation of the client, on my first trip I stayed at the Connaught Hotel, a historic place populated by high-level foreign dignitaries and other people of importance. After walking down the open staircase to breakfast, I was stopped by the maître d' dressed in a formal morning coat, who politely told me I could not enter the breakfast room without a suit and tie. I decided I would try a different hotel on my next trip. Thereafter, I would stay at the Savoy, another historic hotel, near the theater district. Adjusting my routine on future trips, I would fly on a conventional plane, arrive in London in the early evening, drop off my luggage, and walk to Orso, a restaurant in the theater district. I would be ready for business the next morning after an English breakfast at the Savoy overlooking the River Thames.

As we moved into the discovery phase of the revived litigation, the defendants sought to take the deposition of the director of the offshore Jersey subsidiary of ADT that had purchased the defendant's securities. This person was an employee of a bank in Saint Helier, the capital of Jersey in the Channel Islands. I made arrangements to fly to London and then change planes for a shorter flight to Jersey. Located off the coast of France but historically British-controlled, this island has an otherworldly quality. Deplaning on a ramp, I was motioned aside by a man who flashed a badge and began to question me. What was I doing there? What was the nature of my business? Apparently satisfied with my answers, he allowed me to clear immigration, and I took a taxi to my hotel, which looked out over a harbor and bay about two miles long with a castle in the distance. Over a period of hours, I could witness the sea advancing and receding with a mile or more of the sea bottom alternately being exposed or hidden by the tide.

My mission was to meet the bank officer for dinner. Since I arrived several hours early, I asked my taxi driver to give me a tour of the island, which he told me could easily be completed within two hours or so. It was fascinating to drive around an island that seemed frozen in time with an obvious British culture and remnants of a French community as well. I met my dinner companion at a rustic restaurant, conducted my predeposition interview, and flew back to the United States the next morning. Before I left, he gave me a tour of his office at the bank, in which there was a room with dozens of brass plates displaying the names of the offshore "shelf companies" for which he was responsible, including the ADT subsidiary.

It was a year later in the progress of discovery that an event occurred that would be the fulfillment of any litigator's fantasy.

The time came for the defendant to produce documents in London, where I and my associate would visit the office of the defendant's lawyers. When we arrived, we were ushered into a conference room, where we were greeted by a polite English lawyer who offered us tea and then showed us where documents had been placed in neat piles, with a cover sheet with handwritten numbers to correspond to each number of our document request. The document review could be accomplished in three or four hours.

Left alone in the conference room, my colleague and I began to get an overview of the documents, mentally sorting out the most important ones to review first. We sat there silently and spent a couple of hours reading the documents. Then we came across one that immediately caught our attention. It was a report prepared for the company's Chairman. The document set forth details of catastrophic problems that certain of the company's operations had experienced. These were the problems that had been identified by the company in the public releases that led to the cratering of its stock price. But what this report showed was that the company was aware of these significant problems long before their public disclosure. This went to the heart of our case.

As we reviewed this report, we saw that it had been prepared by somebody consulted by the company whom we believed to be a lawyer (and it was marked "Confidential"), but the report itself made clear to us that the author was not providing legal advice. And the document had been freely produced to us along with the other documents. This reinforced our thinking that the defendant's lawyer themselves did not believe the document was legally privileged. Had there been a basis to believe that the production of the document was inadvertent, it might have posed a dilemma, as the rules guiding a lawyer's conduct upon being furnished with a privileged document vary in different jurisdictions. Here, it did not appear to us that there was an "inadvertent production," but rather a knowing and deliberate one. But to reinforce our conclusion, we asked the lawyer hosting us to make copies of several documents, including this one, handing her no more than four or five documents. She readily obliged by going to the copy machine and providing the requested copies. This confirmed two things: First, it confirmed our belief that there was no inadvertent production of a purportedly privileged document; and second, it meant that we would have a copy of it in case the defendant, in a less-than-honest afterthought, might claim privilege when it later appreciated the significance of the document. That is exactly what happened. Back in the States, we included the memo in a filing in the court. The defendant cried foul, claiming an inadvertent production of a privileged document. Reviewing all the facts, the District Judge agreed with us that the document was not privileged.

Toward the end of the discovery period, it became time for the defendant to take the deposition of the Chairman of ADT, Lord Michael Ashcroft. He was a well-known figure in the UK, not only a billionaire but deeply involved in politics, including a term as Deputy Chairman of the Conservative Party. He was recognized as a leading citizen of Belize, where he retained his citizenship while he spent most of his time on his yacht cruising the world. I assumed this provided him tax benefits and also allowed him to spend time in various places as a diplomat of Belize.

I accompanied Ashcroft to his deposition in lower Manhattan. After an hour or two of testimony, he received a call on his cellphone, and he asked to be excused to take the call in a private room. I accompanied him to the separate room and listened while he took a call from Dennis Kozlowski, the Chairman of

Tyco, and Mark Swartz, Tyco's Chief Financial Officer. In the middle of this deposition, they were negotiating the merger of ADT and Tyco. Little did I know at the time that Kozlowski and Swartz would later be indicted and, after trial, spend time in a New York state prison.

Toward the end of the deposition, the opposing lawyer asked Ashcroft whether he could stay a little longer for further questioning, as she knew Ashcroft would be flying back to London. He said it was no problem. Little did she know that awaiting him was his own private jet with a full staff to fly him home at his convenience.

In order for the ADT/Tyco merger to take place, as often happens in these situations, it was important to get this litigation resolved. It was accomplished with a couple of phone calls and after years of litigation, it was over.

CHAPTER 37

JUDGING THE JUDGES

The Appellate Division of the New York State Supreme Court is one of the most important courts in the State and the nation in the field of commercial law. The Court is divided into four geographical Departments that hear appeals from the Supreme Court (the highest trial-level court) and some other courts in New York's sixty-two counties. Only a small fraction of the cases decided by the Appellate Division are reviewed by the New York Court of Appeals, the State's highest court. Therefore, for most litigants, the Appellate Division has the final word.

Appellate Division Justices are chosen by the Governor from applicants who are already elected Supreme Court Justices. However, those seeking promotion to the appellate court do not apply directly to the Governor. Under an executive order that has remained in place over many gubernatorial administrations, a Judicial Screening Committee is in place in each of the four Departments. The committee members are chosen by the Governor, the State's Attorney General, and leaders in the Legislature. When Andrew Cuomo (who later became Governor) was elected Attorney General, he appointed me to the Judicial Screening Committee for the Second Department, in which I reside; when he became Governor, Cuomo, at my request, appointed me to the Screening Committee for the First Department in Manhattan, where I maintain my principal office.

The screening process is an excellent one. It combines features of both merit selection and political responsiveness: The lawyers on the committee are charged with ensuring that the best available candidates are presented to the Governor (with a binary rating system of either Highly Qualified or Not Highly Qualified). The Governor also weighs the requests by political leaders in the different counties to have candidates from their regions considered for the promotion. The screening process is rigorous, and over the eighteen years I have been involved with it, I have learned a lot about the perspectives of judges who serve the public. Candidates from different backgrounds and perspectives ensure that litigants receive the fairest treatment. Since the Appellate Division hears appeals involving subjects ranging from divorce law to commercial matters, and both civil and criminal matters, having judges on the court with prior experience in different areas of the law is particularly helpful.

CHAPTER 38

CAMERAS IN THE COURTS

Over the past several decades, the American public has been offered a master class in how trials and other legal proceedings are conducted. Beyond the likes of television shows such as *Judge Judy*, most states now allow television coverage of trials, or parts of them, sometimes shielding certain participants such as jurors from public view. Federal courts lag way behind these developments, reflecting not only a general conservatism, but lingering concerns about the effect of television coverage on the fairness of the proceeding.

Between 1987 and 1997, New York State experimented with allowing television coverage of trials through a series of legislative enactments, but New York does not permit full coverage today. Each legislative enactment had a so-called "sunset provision" that made the authorization expire after a certain period of time. These laws suspended, but now leave in place, Section 52 of the New York Civil Rights Law which prohibits the "televising, broadcasting, or taking of motion pictures" of New York State court proceedings in which witnesses' testimony is or may be taken.

Over twenty years ago, the President of the New York Bar Association created a Special Committee, on which I served, to look at this issue. Its members included trial lawyers of various stripes, as well as those representing television and print media. We took testimony from a wide range of persons with an interest in the subject of television coverage. We heard from, among others, prosecutors, criminal defense lawyers, judges, and jurors. At the end of our work, we recommended that New York once again lift its ban on television coverage. Principally motivating our recommendation was that there is a significant public interest in having widely accessible coverage of trials (there is already a bedrock principle in our justice system that trials should be public). Moreover, the public's ability to see court proceedings remotely can make more understandable, and therefore legitimize, the results of a trial that would otherwise not be understood and accepted. One example we discussed was a not-guilty verdict in a high-profile case in New York City in which police officers were charged with shooting and killing an innocent civilian, Amadou Diallo. The testifying defendant police officers' testimony, in which they expressed remorse and even shed tears, was said to have played a large role in the decision to acquit. Most members of our committee also felt the worldwide television coverage of the O. J. Simpson trial in California, despite its theatrics, was of benefit to the public.

On the other side of the issue, perhaps surprisingly, were not only criminal-defense lawyers, but some prosecutors. The defense lawyers complained of instances in which the media would selectively show news clips of a defendant in his worst moments at arraignment or at trial. One prosecutor who frequently brought cases against gang members objected to television coverage because witnesses in the community would be reluctant to testify against them. She said that even the ability to pixelate, thereby distorting, the faces of witnesses would not be effective to protect them, since gang members could still readily determine the identity of the witness. New York's prohibition on cameras in the court has recently received renewed attention in the criminal and civil trials of Donald J. Trump. New York remains somewhat of an outlier by restricting televised testimony of trials. It is unclear what the future will hold.

CHAPTER 39

MANDATORY RETIREMENT OF LAWYERS

Twenty years ago, the President of the New York State Bar Association asked me to chair a Special Committee to look at a common practice of major law firms: mandatory retirement of partners based on age. A look at this practice was prompted by changes over time not only in the law profession but in society at large. People are living longer than they did generations ago, and with that there is often the financial need, as well as the desire, to continue to work. On the national level, Congress recognized this some time ago and enacted legislation to outlaw as a form of age discrimination, with certain exceptions, mandatory retirement in most businesses in the United States.

Many major law firms traditionally followed mandatory retirement practices, sometimes setting an age limit of as young as fifty-five or sixty. Law firms justified this on the grounds that partners reaching those ages had benefited from the retirement of those who came before them and that it was only fair to make room for the financial advancement of younger partners. Underlying this justification was the notion that there is a financial "pie" of fixed dimension—the annual earnings of the firm—and that only by requiring mandatory retirement can these fixed resources be fairly allocated.

At the time our committee began its work, the law was unsettled as to whether partners in law firms were "employees" or "employers"; only the former would be subject to the protections of the federal age discrimination laws. Our committee did not attempt to resolve that legal issue. Rather, we examined some of the underlying assumptions used to justify mandatory retirement in the law-firm setting. First, we observed that that concept of a fixed "pie" was not entirely accurate. Many lawyers with years of experience had client relationships that would continue more reliably if the partner were not mandatorily retired. At the same time, at a certain age, the partner might be happy to take less compensation while continuing to perform the valuable role of liaison between the client and other lawyers in the firm doing the client's work. That partner might also provide valuable service by training and mentoring younger lawyers.

A second reason for doing away with mandatory retirement was that even when an older lawyer produced less revenue, if he or she assumed the status of counsel or senior counsel rather than partner, any decreased profitability of such lawyers as a group would not reduce the "profit per partner" statistic that today publications such as *The American Lawyer* make public. This statistic is important to law firms, because it is one metric that is used to attract lawyers from other firms. Finally, and perhaps most interestingly, we made the observation that perhaps the most powerful dynamic that motivates law firms to retain a policy of mandatory retirement is not economic but stems from a reluctance to grant exceptions to highly productive lawyers while declining to grant them to others. That is a very uncomfortable situation for law firms that try to maintain a modicum of cordiality in an environment in which reducing stress is an important objective.

Our Special Committee report concluded with a recommendation that the practice of mandatory retirement be discontinued. Our report was adopted by the House of Delegates of the New York State Bar Association, which made it the official position of the Association. The report was then presented to the leadership of the American Bar Association, which adopted it as well. While today, some law firms have abandoned the policy of mandatory retirement, others still maintain it. In the absence of a definitive ruling from the U.S. Supreme Court on whether partners in law firms are employers or employees, the practice will likely continue for the time being. If the Court were to issue a definitive ruling, many commentators believe it would take an approach similar to that which it has taken in other situations in which age discrimination laws apply. If it does so, it would likely require a trial court to determine in any particular case whether the partner claiming age discrimination enjoyed the essential attributes of a participating decision-maker, or whether the law firm was so centrally managed and administered that the partner was essentially an employee. At some point, we will likely have clarity.

CHAPTER 40
MAKING MISTAKES

Nobody likes to make mistakes. But they happen to everybody, and they can be the best learning tool. When I was a young associate, I would sometimes be a fly on the wall as the "sophomore" lawyers (those who were not neophytes but not senior) would talk about mistakes made by adversaries in their litigations. Listening to this, I wondered whether if I made a mistake, I would be subject to the same ridicule or worse, find that my job was in jeopardy. Somewhere along the way, I learned that my concern about making an error could actually inhibit my professional growth.

Elsewhere in this book, I have recounted my efforts to participate with well-known lawyers in continuing legal-education programs. I would typically design the program, moderate it, and have as panelists some of the best-known litigators in New York City and elsewhere. On occasion, our panel presented the program in more than one city. We typically would fly to the city where the program would be presented and share a drink in the hotel bar on the night before the program. I recall that one night Milton Gould, a larger-than-life trial lawyer for decades, regaled us with "war stories" of cases he had tried going back to the 1930s. A prominent theme in these stories, which were filled with humor, was the mistakes Gould had made along the way. Although Gould had an understandably large ego, he seemed to get the most pleasure out of his stories about the "screw-ups" that attended some of his trials. I learned a lesson from that. If the great Milton Gould could endure these mistakes and still achieve great prominence, maybe my concerns were misplaced.

Decades later, I, too, enjoy recounting such instances when I meet with younger lawyers. I recall over thirty years ago trying a jury case in Nassau County on Long Island. The client, a widow, had been married to a man who, during the Depression, had worked in a small company on the West Side of Manhattan. This company had a niche business supplying the major producers of electrical cables with something called paper folders—insulation that was applied under the rubber insulation of outdoor electrical cables. The company had a good relationship with perhaps a dozen of the major cable companies. After many years, the original owner retired and the client's husband purchased the business, paying the owner what he could afford over a period of years.

After many years of running this small but successful company, the widow's husband was diagnosed with cancer. He went through a series of treatments and during the short period of remission, he tried to resume work, slowly walking up the three flights of steep stairs in the old building where the company was housed. Eventually, he could do it no more.

One of the key employees was the nephew of the original owner and bore the same last name. They carried on the business while the widow's husband was ill. When the husband died, the widow, who had not worked for many years, visited the business and went through the bookkeeping records. It turned out that in the past couple of years, the company had lost half of its customers. She could not understand it. So, she called one of the customers and was told that they had received instructions to send payments to a different address but to the same company name. Of course, the nephew bore the same last name as did the founder of the company. He and a cohort had been manufacturing the paper folders in his basement and instructing the customers to send payment to that address.

The widow brought suit against the two perfidious employees. I was asked to replace her lawyer when the time came for the trial. In New York State courts, as I have discussed elsewhere in this book, unlike the procedure in most states and in federal courts, the lawyers for the parties in a civil case are permitted to question prospective jurors without the presence of a judge. The applicable rules permit the lawyer for each party to ask wide-ranging questions to determine if a prospective juror can be fair and unbiased. In particular, a rule allows the lawyers to explain what their "contentions" are. This generally opens the door for a lawyer to summarize the facts that will be presented, in the hope that their questioning will influence the jurors before the trial even begins. I tried exactly that.

I began by explaining to those assembled what I just described, then mentioning how painful it was for the husband to be spending his last days struggling to walk up those stairs to do what he had done for so many years. The evidence would show the terrible disloyalty of key employees who took advantage of this circumstance—and the widow's attempt to save the business. When I finished, I asked the group of prospective jurors, "Now that you have heard what our contentions are, if there is anyone who feels they cannot be fair and impartial in this case, please raise your hand." Three quarters of the people raised their hands.

As is the required procedure, we asked each of them individually to step out of the room along with the lawyers on both sides. I asked the first one, "Why is it that you couldn't be fair and impartial?" The woman responded, "That story you told is so horrible, and what the employee did is so terrible, I could not possibly be fair and impartial." Well, each person who had raised their hand that we questioned gave essentially the same response. So, the result was that by my saying too much during the *voir dire* process, I lost the opportunity to have on the jury some of the people who would be most sympathetic to my client. Fortunately, we had a favorable verdict that included both compensatory and punitive damages. But I learned a lesson that I will not forget.

Perhaps the most serious mistake lawyers make is in dealings with their clients. It is an area in which experienced lawyers typically have much better judgment than those who are less experienced. And it is a particular problem area for litigators. A lawyer who undertakes to prepare a will or a corporate agreement, or to handle a real-estate transaction, can fairly well estimate how much time will be required and offer a client a fixed fee or provide an estimate that is close to the actual time expended. Litigation is different. Estimating the time that will be required is like trying to predict at the beginning of a war where the skirmishes will be fought, what ordnance will be required, how many troops will be casualties, how long the war will take, and what the outcome will be. I have frequently asked lawyers the following question: Considering all the times in your career that you have estimated for a client legal fees for a prospective litigation, and taking into account both the overestimation and underestimation you have provided, what is the "net"? Every lawyer I have spoken with has told me they have consistently underestimated and virtually never overestimated the time that they would actually spend on the matter.

This dynamic often lays the groundwork for disputes with clients. While clients may understand that it is impossible to predict the cost of litigation, they will resent receiving bills that reflect fees that are a multiple of what the lawyer originally estimated. This often leads to a breakdown of trust between lawyer and client. In some cases, when lawyers feel they have no option but to bring litigation against the client to collect a fee, a client responds with a claim of legal malpractice, whether or not it has merit. Lawyers who make the mistake of not billing regularly and addressing payment problems immediately increase the prospect of adversity with the client.

Another critical feature of the lawyer-client relationship is perceiving the fuzzy line between areas that are the prerogative of the client and that of the lawyer. I sometimes posit the analogy of the surgeon who plans to perform an operation. It is certainly up to the patient or his family to have input into the nature and scope of the operation. However, once that is agreed upon, the patient does not stand in the operating room dictating precisely where the surgeon places the scalpel. Lawyers who fail to appreciate this distinction set themselves up for trouble.

A skill that often takes lawyers time to develop is knowing which clients not to take. This is difficult, because lawyers are not in practice to refuse representations. But there are often signs at the very outset that the lawyer should avoid the prospective client. A controlling personality, unrealistic expectations, or a demand for a fee discount are all red flags that should alert the lawyer to potential problems. This is particularly important because even when there is a breakdown in the lawyer-client relationship, lawyers have a professional responsibility to protect a client's interest in withdrawing, as well as to obtain court permission, which may not always be granted.

CHAPTER 41

ALTERNATIVE DISPUTE RESOLUTION

Beginning in the 1950s, arbitration emerged as an alternative to court litigation to resolve business disputes. The business community saw the possibility of reducing the costs of litigation, as well as the prospect of having arbitrators with specialized knowledge of their industry resolve disputes. Accordingly, it became increasingly common for businesses to include arbitration clauses in their contracts. At the same time, organizations such as the American Arbitration Association, with its roster of arbitrators, expanded to serve the business community.

Historians have observed that the Holy Roman Empire was neither holy, Roman, nor an empire. So too it has been said that arbitration has not turned out to be either fair, efficient, or inexpensive. There are several reasons for this. For one, arbitrators, unlike judges, are compensated by the parties, some of whom are not motivated to make efficiency a priority. Moreover, while some disputes require the assignment of only one arbitrator, many arbitrations are conducted by three arbitrators, each of whom is paid by the parties. And one of the principles inherent in the arbitration process is that only in unusual circumstances will a court disturb the arbitrator's decisions on appeal (such as where bias or corruption is shown to have cast doubt on the legitimacy of the award). It is not even common that an award is overturned for the arbitrator's "manifest disregard of the law."

Although these principles are intended to impart efficiency to the arbitration process, in reality the arbitrator's issuance of an award at the conclusion of the proceeding often does not end the matter. The party seeking to enforce the award has to apply to a court (in New York State, the Supreme Court), where the party opposing the award locks horns with the adversary in what is essentially an appellate proceeding. And when that court renders its decision, the aggrieved party has an appeal to a higher court. Finally, while arbitration proceedings originally imparted efficiency by restricting the scope and extent of pretrial discovery (such as eliminating most depositions of witnesses and pretrial motions), in recent decades, expanded discovery in arbitration has become much more common. It is probably for many of these reasons that the field of mediation, which I turn to next, has expanded as a better alternative.

There is a familiar saying in this developing field: An ounce of mediation is worth a pound of arbitration and a ton of litigation. Not only has law evolved to resolve disputes more fairly, so has the process itself for doing so. Many disputes present close issues, where right and wrong is hazy, not clear. Each party to a dispute can often point to factors, both legal and factual, that favor its position.

The process of adjudication in both courts and in arbitration is generally binary: Somebody wins and somebody loses.

The virtue of "alternative dispute resolution"—most commonly some form of mediation—is that it puts aside the notion of winners and losers and tries to produce a consensual resolution. It is imperfect, but it has great potential benefits for all parties. Mediation has achieved such popularity that many national and local conflict-resolution firms have made a business of providing mediation services. In fact, the process has become so prevalent that courts and bar associations have enlisted volunteers, typically retired judges and experienced lawyers, to provide these services without charge. This is yet another example of the willingness of professionals to contribute to the community.

There are several features that often make mediation successful. Aside from the obvious virtue of compromise, the mediation process allows parties to feel their grievance has been heard and acknowledged. Even with complex and high-stakes business disputes, there is an emotional and human component that drives the parties. A good mediator recognizes this.

Mediation also has a virtue that is not present in litigation. Often the parties have a continuing business relationship, or at least the prospect of one, that can help produce a solution. If a financial resolution of the current dispute can be achieved, preserving the relationship on an ongoing basis can be a benefit to the parties. In addition, in litigation, communications between lawyers and judges without direct client involvement are generally the determinants of the outcome. In contrast, mediators generally require the principals themselves to be present and participate in the settlement process. Where useful, the mediator may also encourage the principals to listen to the arguments of the opposing lawyer rather than hear them only through the voice of their own lawyer.

Some decades ago, when I first became involved in representing clients in mediation, I was often skeptical of the likelihood of a positive outcome. On many occasions, I have been pleasantly surprised. As I became more involved, acting as a mediator myself, I gained a great deal of professional satisfaction in helping to resolve a dispute that seemed intractable.

The mechanics of the mediation process are varied and in fact almost infinite. Parties can begin the process with no prior agreement as to the range of possibilities; or they might agree in advance to a "bracket" for the process, which means any negotiation will involve "numbers" between the agreed floor and ceiling. Also, when there is a binary financial problem—that is, how much one party will pay—there can also be an agreement to discuss other aspects of potential disputes that can be resolved. For example, if one party claims a copyright or trademark right has been violated, the comprehensive agreement might involve sharing of revenue generated by future exploitation of that right, together with resolution of other open issues. An imaginative and creative mediator can often suggest points for resolution that the parties themselves have not thought about.

Going forward, I would predict that, given the inevitable cost and inherent uncertainty of litigation, more and more parties to disputes will appreciate the value of crafting their own settlement, knowing that when they conclude the mediation, the matter is settled once and for all. No more will they incur the expenditure of legal fees on trials and appeals that will require the parties to spend money for an indeterminate time to come.

CHAPTER 42

LOOKING THROUGH THE OTHER END OF THE TELESCOPE

One of the most valuable experiences a lawyer can have is serving as an arbitrator, or as in an unusual situation that I encountered, serving as the equivalent of a judge. Although I had practiced law for decades as an advocate, it was only after I had been afforded the chance to "look through the other end of the telescope" that I came to appreciate how decision-makers view lawyers' arguments. Perhaps the most significant lesson I learned is that to be optimally effective as an advocate, you have to think about the case not as you see it, but as a neutral third person will likely view it. The two views are not necessarily the same. At every stage of the litigation process, from the time you draft the complaint through the pretrial phase and the trial and any appeal, we must keep this in mind.

There is another development that has helped me gain this perspective. In today's world of commercial litigation, particularly when the stakes are high, we typically retain consultants to give us an opportunity to try a condensed version of our case before either a retired judge or a group of individuals chosen to replicate the local jury pool as closely as possible. We do the same thing when anticipating arguing an appeal before a panel of judges. This process is not intended to predict the outcome of a case. Rather, it is designed to help us identify and evaluate the issues that are likely to be outcome-determinative in our upcoming court presentations. In fact, in considering which retired judges we should retain for our mock exercises, we sometimes reject a candidate who we know has very strong views, in favor of another candidate with less conviction. This is because what is important to us is not the judge's personal view of the case, but that person's ability to predict the view of the actual judge or judges who will hear the case. It may sound like a fine distinction, but it is an important one.

The case that has brought home to me the importance of objectivity is an unusual one—a dispute that has been litigated before me for the last ten years, in which I have replaced the Supreme Court Justice assigned to the case. Beginning in the fall of 2014, Mr. Paul Napoli and Mr. Marc Bern, the two principals of a highly successful plaintiffs' personal injury and mass-tort law firm, engaged in acrimonious litigation against one another in New York relating to the breakup of their law firm. The dispute spilled into the public press and created problems for them professionally and for their law firm. The two lawyers brought numerous motions before the New York Supreme Court, seeking rulings almost weekly on the many issues that arose as a consequence of their personal feud and the difficulties of administering a law firm under these circumstances. At one point, the trial judge appointed a Receiver to oversee the affairs of the Napoli Bern firm, but he was later relieved of his responsibilities, and I was appointed as Referee to act in place of the Supreme Court Justice overseeing this litigation, acting with the powers of the Supreme Court. Here is how that evolved:

In July 2015, with Messrs. Napoli and Bern unable to resolve their disputes and the litigation continuing, the trial judge suggested to the parties that they attempt to mediate their disputes under my supervision. The parties thereafter contacted me and engaged in a multi-day mediation process to attempt to resolve all issues. The mediation did not succeed, but at the parties' request, my role then became an entirely different one.

The parties realized that resolving the issues confronting them as they worked to unwind a firm of this size—which was representing more than twenty thousand clients—would be an enormous task that could not be accomplished quickly or easily. Represented by experienced and able counsel, the parties worked out the terms of a settlement agreement and a side-letter agreement that were essentially an operating manual for the issues that needed to be addressed, in what was envisioned to be a lengthy unwinding process. Central to that agreement was the parties' proposal that I would personally adjudicate all of the disputes between them.

To effectuate this proposal, the parties asked that I be appointed as a Referee to hear and determine all issues between them "with all the powers of the Court." In effect, they retained me as a "private judge" to operate within the court system. They incorporated terms in their agreement that authorized me to undertake numerous responsibilities and to make certain determinations that went beyond the scope of their existing pleadings.

The parties contemplated that I would be substituted for the trial judge, so that any appeals from my orders would be taken directly to the Appellate Division of Supreme Court. Among other things, the agreement provided that:

- "The parties have agreed to petition the Court…for the appointment of Mark C. Zauderer (the 'Referee') as the referee in the Supreme Court Action to hear and determine, with all the powers of the Court available to him, including, but not limited to, those under CPLR §4301—including, without limitation, subpoena powers, power to decide financial disputes between the parties arising under the terms of this Agreement and contempt powers under the CPLR, and the power to resolve disputes concerning the Firm's litigation strategy where the Firm is a named party";
- "[A]ny dispute or controversy arising under or in connection with this Agreement, the Supreme Court Action, and/or any aspect of the global dispute between the undersigned, shall be decided or determined by the Referee";
- "[T]he Referee shall be charged with overseeing the winding down of the Firm and an orderly transition to the [parties'] New Firms";
- "The Referee has the power to direct the reimbursement of all costs of any legal action or claim brought to the Referee and/or referred to the Court, including the Referee's fees and expenses, reasonable attorney's fees and expenses, accountant's fees and expenses, and fees associated with the enforcement of this Agreement";

- "The degree, nature, and timing of [the parties'] cooperation is subject to…Zauderer's strict oversight";
- "The parties, with Zauderer's oversight, will create separate Lockboxes for the Firm based on the Firm's structure," and that "Zauderer will resolve any disputes" with respect to the creation and maintenance of the Lockbox;
- "[T]he Referee, after briefing and presentations made by both parties, shall determine the specific NB QM gates that dictate the NB QM Fee for each of the respective Firms";
- "[T]o the extent there is disagreement [about the Firm's third-party debt], the Referee shall determine which creditors and the amounts are to be authorized";
- Because neither party should pay "more than 50% of the debt recorded on the Firm's books or otherwise owed by the Firm," I would oversee a periodic and final true-up process between the parties, including making adjustments to the parties' "quantum meruit" percentages when necessary; and
- If, subsequent to the division and allocation of the legacy firm's more than twenty thousand clients, a client changed from one party to the other, or if one party made an effort to solicit clients allocated to the other, "Zauderer may make an appropriate financial adjustment."

The agreement was presented for approval to the trial judge. It expressly conditioned the settlement on the Court's entering an order appointing me in the pending action as a Referee to hear and determine "with all the powers of the Court." Under the CPLR (New York's civil procedure code), any appeals from orders of a Supreme Court referee to "hear and determine," like those of the Supreme Court Justice, are taken directly to the Appellate Division of the Supreme Court. The trial court issued such an order on August 17, 2015. By its terms, the order incorporated by reference the parties' Settlement Agreement, and the Court appointed me "to serve as the referee in this Action and to have the powers to hear and determine all issues related to this Action, with all the powers of the Court available to him, including, but not limited to, those under CPLR §§ 4301 and 4317," with "all immunities or protections at law" afforded to me by virtue of the appointment.

Since the entry of the order appointing me as Referee, over the last decade, the principals or their counsel have met with me in person, telephonically or, more recently, via Zoom, on dozens of occasions, to address the many issues confronting them in the effort to wind down the affairs of the legacy Napoli Bern firm in an orderly manner. Many issues have been resolved by me, either through forging agreement of the parties or by making rulings resolving disagreements. I have issued more than seventy written orders, including scheduling orders and decisions addressing the merits of disputed issues, and I have made many dozens of rulings orally on the record during our in-person, telephonic, or Zoom conferences.

One illustration of the utility of this "private judge" arrangement is an emergency that was presented to me late one Friday afternoon in the summer. I was onboard *Different Drummer* off the coast of Connecticut when I received an email advising me there was a dispute between Messrs. Napoli and Bern that needed to be resolved quickly. Their firm had a deadline of Monday morning to make an application for legal fees in Chicago in a large settlement involving millions of dollars. They disagreed as to the amount of legal fees to be sought. I ordered a remote hearing to be held the next day with a court reporter on the telephone to record the proceedings. At the appointed time on Saturday afternoon, I convened the telephone hearing and began by stating on the record that I was aboard my boat in the harbor at Mamaroneck, New York. I noted that because I was now within the jurisdiction of New York State, I could issue orders from that location. I then heard the arguments and immediately issued a decision so that the fee application could be timely submitted to the court in Chicago on Monday morning.

Over the years, I have served as an arbitrator in significant cases for the American Arbitration Association and its related International Centre for Dispute Resolution. In one case, our panel of three arbitrators heard a dispute between two contractors who supplied all the food to United States troops in Iraq and Afghanistan. In another case, a different panel on which I served heard a dispute between an NFL football team and a major university. In yet another arbitration, a three-arbitrator panel of which I was a member heard a dispute between a major soft drink manufacturer and its supplier of aluminum cans.

These and other cases for which I have served as an arbitrator illustrate the diversity of subject matter that a decision-maker hears. For a litigator, having the opportunity to hear lawyers argue and "look through the other end of the telescope" is an immensely valuable experience. It helps us as advocates to make more objective judgments in choosing the issues we present to the court and the way we argue them.

CHAPTER 43

WHAT HAS HAPPENED TO LAW FIRMS?

The large law firm of today bears only a slight resemblance to what it was fifty years ago. When I joined Kaye Scholer as an associate, I was the 110th lawyer to join that firm. It was comparable in size to other major New York City law firms. Today, of course, similar firms number their lawyers in the thousands.

Understanding these changes requires taking into account a number of shifts in both the business and social culture of law firms. Fifty years ago, the major law firms were largely homegrown affairs. Many if not most of the young associates looked to the firm not only to give them training but, if they performed well, to give them a track to a coveted partnership after eight or nine years of devoted service. Those who became partners expected they would remain at the firm for decades until retirement. Those who were "passed over" often were placed in in-house legal positions with institutional clients of the law firm.

As has been widely observed, the legal profession was dominated by male lawyers whose spouses often gave up work to concentrate on family responsibilities. A half day of Saturday work was routine at the law firm, with both lawyers and staff working until lunchtime. Many lawyers would then go out to lunch with a senior partner and eventually arrive home late Saturday afternoon. The law firm also encouraged lawyers to join bar associations, where they would participate in the evening in projects of interest to the profession.

Each year in most firms, an associate lawyer would receive a review by a senior partner assigned to the task. The comments about the lawyer's work would be synthesized by the reviewer who would summarize the good and sometimes the less good; the associate whose work was generally thought to be of good quality would be encouraged, often with a statement that "you are on the right track." This deliberate ambiguity would be designed to encourage the associate to keep working hard in the hope of eventually becoming a partner. The reviewing partner did not refer to the specific number of billable hours the associate had recorded during the past year, but if the number was high, it might draw a favorable comment about the lawyer's commendable efforts.

Over the following decades, a number of changes took place. Through industry publications such as the pioneering *American Lawyer*, partners became aware of how much lawyers at other law firms were earning. At the same time, the stratospheric earnings of contemporaries at investment banks were being widely talked about. Also, law-firm leaders would say that as businesses became more and more global, law firms needed to be larger and operate in more cities to retain these corporate clients.

This confluence of factors was, in my view, the key to understanding how and why law firms changed. They also were responsible for the practice of law evolving from a profession to a business. To put this in perspective, consider that the profession of law, like medicine and accountancy, was once thought to be a learned profession worthy of high respect in the community. The coin of the realm for most professionals was not wealth, but respect and high social status. I am reminded of the image of the doctor who would make house calls to visit sick patients and not return home until every patient had been seen. When was the last time you were paid such a visit?

Beginning in the 1980s, all of these factors led law firms to focus increasingly on the "bottom line" and, relatedly, partner income. There are basically two ways to accomplish greater profitability. Assuming annual increases in fixed costs can be offset by reducing certain other costs, the first way to increase profitability is increasing lawyer billing rates and relatedly requiring lawyers to bill more hours. Each year, firm management would formulate a budget—very much as businesses do—with profitability in the coming year to be increased by an arbitrary percentage. Then, the internal accountants would calculate how many billed hours and at what increased rates would allow the firm to meet this goal. This would require a plan to have lawyers, particularly associates, bill more hours. These additional billed hours are particularly profitable for law firms because the overhead of the firm, including lawyers' salaries, is largely fixed.

To achieve these increased hour goals, firms needed to incentivize lawyers to bill more hours. They did this by establishing a minimum number of expected hours coupled with a bonus if the lawyer reached a predetermined target, such as two thousand hours for the year. Needless to say, these defined expectations create a potential for abuse (sometimes referred to as "padding" hours) that is difficult to monitor, particularly because there is not a great incentive to do so. These changes did not go unnoticed by sophisticated clients. In an effort to address potentially inefficient billing, many corporate clients have developed extensive and detailed guidelines for the billing practices of the law firms they retained. The net result of these changes has contributed significantly to a diminution in the trust and special relationship that clients and their lawyers once enjoyed.

The second important initiative that firms undertook to increase profitability was to expand their footprint into different cities and even different countries. The often-stated goal was to be able to better serve international clients who wanted "one-stop shopping" for their varied legal needs in different countries and in cross-border transactions. Law firms were eager to accommodate. But to do this, they had to expand their partnership ranks in ways different from the traditional one. Historically, when the major corporate law firms operated in one city, such as New York City, they did not hire lawyers who had been out of law school for many years, preferring to grow their ranks by hiring lawyers right out of law school or judicial clerkships to initiate them in the culture of the firm and teach its practices. By the time the lawyers had reached the level to be considered for partnership, they were thoroughly immersed in the law-firm culture, and the firm could be assured of both their competence and loyalty to the firm.

But this traditional model did not work for achieving the expansion the firms were committed to. Instead, the firms would attempt to connect with other firms, or groups within those firms, with an eye towards acquiring those practices. That, in turn, required the acquiring law firm to analyze the financial metrics of the practices of being acquired to ensure increased profitability, largely to the exclusion of the other traditional criteria for partnership affiliation, which emphasized firm culture and values, as well as loyalty. The result of this is well known in the profession. Groups of lawyers join a firm with certain financial expectations. If they are not met, because they may have little loyalty to the firm, they may move on again to another firm.

Another consequence of these changes is that within the ever-growing law firms, individual partners have less of a voice in firm management and selection of new partners than once was the case. While in the traditional single-city law firm, the occasional outside candidate for partnership would be introduced to all partners in the new firm, today management decisions are typically tightly controlled by a central executive committee operating much like the executive suite in a large corporation. An email might be sent to hundreds of partners announcing the planned arrival of a dozen new partners on a given day. The message would say that unless a specified percentage of the partners objected, the deal would be done.

These changes have had other consequences. Because clients have become more sensitive to the increasing costs of legal services, the law firms in turn have spent less time and effort in training newer lawyers, because neither the law firm nor the client wants to absorb the cost of the less efficient work of a new lawyer. Also, in this environment, law firms no longer encourage (and some tacitly discourage) bar association activities, because it is difficult for an associate with minimum hours goals to find time for these uncompensated activities.

There is another change in the profession that has required law firms to adapt. Unlike the profession fifty years ago, the ranks of the firms are populated by both men and women, many of whom are sharing work and family responsibilities. These lawyers do not want to or cannot afford to have Saturday business lunches or attend evening bar association meetings. Many are demanding accommodation not only in the form of family leave but the ability to work remotely, especially since that practice became common during the COVID-19 pandemic. Not only does this put pressure on the firms to accommodate, but many of the newer lawyers who join major firms do not have the expectation that they will become partners in the firm. Rather, they are under significant pressure to pay off debt incurred through their law-school years, knowing that after a few years they will move on for one reason or another. Accordingly, associates have more bargaining power than they once had. Many of my colleagues have observed that if they do not accord associate candidates the privilege to work remotely, they will lose out because the candidate will go elsewhere. Of course, to a great extent, lawyers who do not regularly work in an office and have the planned and unplanned opportunities to meet with colleagues miss out on an important aspect of their professional development.

What I have described here is what the legal profession now unabashedly calls the "business" of law—no longer the "profession" of law. The same is true in the accountancy profession. I recall some years ago a television ad during the Super Bowl by a major accounting firm, which boasted, "We are in the business of accounting." I thought to myself, "Wasn't this once a profession?" I am not sure it will be too long before doctors, too, will see themselves this way. Their ads so prevalent on buses and subways in New York City will soon boast "We are in the business of medicine." And with that, these remaining professionals will join the ranks of businesses.

As of this writing, recent events have brought into focus how much the "business of law" has come to define the legal profession. The current President, Donald J. Trump, has openly declared that he seeks "retribution" against prosecutors and other lawyers who he believes have wrongly investigated or prosecuted him, and on law firms that have supported or hired these lawyers. The President has also committed to eradicating "diversity, equity, and inclusion" programs in law firms and ensuring that *pro bono* work undertaken by lawyers is not limited to supporting favored political causes. Many law firms have widely advertised these initiatives as reflecting the firm's "core values," including DEI, and have cited them in their efforts to recruit talented lawyers graduating from law school or finishing judicial clerkships.

In a series of executive orders (and in several cases threatened or prospective executive orders) issued by the Administration, several targeted law firms were denied access to federal facilities to represent their clients in dealings with the federal government. The orders also directed federal agencies to cancel contracts with these law firms where legally possible. Several of these firms immediately entered into agreements with the Administration to eliminate their DEI policies and devote as much as $40 million (in the case of one firm) and $100 million (in the case of other firms threatened with the executive orders) to *pro bono* programs that support causes favored by the Administration. Some of these law firms have scrubbed any biographical material mentioning the work of their partners who had served as prosecutors investigating or prosecuting the President from their websites. Some lawyers (as well as some opinion writers) have criticized as "capitulation" the firms' agreeing to the Administration's demands; others have acknowledged the firms' understandable concern that their clients (as well as important partners) would desert the firms if the executive orders were implemented—which firms have characterized as "existential threats" to their survival.

While some law firms have agreed to the Administration's terms, several other major firms have brought lawsuits and have obtained temporary restraining orders prohibiting implementation of the Administration's executive orders. The firms have asserted that these executive orders are unconstitutional, as they restrict the firms and their clients in advocating in court against the government or negotiating transactions with it. Currently, the litigation outcomes are uncertain.

Whether one approves or disapproves of the steps the Administration has taken, these events demonstrate how the business concerns of law firms have in many cases been given priority over what they themselves have advertised as "core values," such as DEI and *pro bono* work. In their view, the survival of the firm, including retaining clients who are apprehensive about retaining a law firm at odds with the government, is priority number one. And their own public statements explaining their rationale for complying with the government's demands simply punctuate the point that law-firm priorities today are the business of law.

But the current focus on the business of law has obscured other changes in the profession. These have impacted the work quality of some major law firms, at least in the area with which I am most familiar: litigation. Here is a peek into that world.

As most nonlawyers know, writing legal briefs is a chief tool of advocates. In a typical legal argument, the lawyer brings to the attention of the court the so-called "precedents" of similar cases. Depending upon whether a particular precedent the lawyer cites is merely "persuasive" or "controlling" (meaning the court must follow it, if applicable), the lawyer will argue that the court should follow it, to the advantage of his or her client.

When I started law practice, I would draft a legal brief for review by the partner supervising the matter. He or she would ask me to provide not only the draft brief but also copies of the cases I cited to support my argument. The partner would then review the draft brief and read the cases, to ensure that the cases really stood for the propositions for which they were cited. The partner would then meet with me in person to ensure that, if necessary, the brief was modified. This process is essential if a litigator is not to lose credibility with the court.

An inexperienced litigator usually does not know the subtleties of using case citations effectively. For example, the facts recited in the cited precedent may be quite different from those involved in the present case. Such a circumstance enables the opposing lawyers to "distinguish" the cited case, arguing that it should have no persuasive force. Moreover, the inexperienced lawyer is likely to treat every possibly relevant case with equal respect and fashion the argument accordingly. Most lawyers know that a higher-court case demands more attention than a lower-court case. However, in citing such a case, one needs to consider a number of factors. What was the setting of the higher court opinion? Did it simply affirm an after-trial decision by the lower court, without providing detailed reasoning (this is often the case where the lower court has made highly discretionary rulings which are not likely to be overturned on appeal, except for an "abuse of discretion")? Also, if the cited decision of the trial court is in a different district or a different court (state versus federal), it might carry with it less weight in the court in which it is cited. Finally, is the case very old? A judge may be less inclined to accept as persuasive a precedent that is 125 years old than a decision that was issued a year ago.

What I have just described has become an increasingly serious problem, because senior lawyers in major firms generally take much less time today reviewing the work product of younger lawyers to provide both professional guidance and to ensure the quality of the work product. Today, clients are much less accepting of paying bills that include associate "training" time on the matter; and law firms are not particularly eager to absorb that cost themselves. In recent years, I have read many briefs from major firms, and in many instances the inapplicability of the precedents cited is fairly obvious.

To be clear: There is still some excellent work done by leading law firms. But in my experience, in the profession there is no longer the consistency of product quality that once was the hallmark of these firms. Unfortunately, a law firm's name attached to a brief no longer guarantees excellence.

CHAPTER 44

LET PROFESSIONALISM BE YOUR GUIDE

Graduating from law school and entering the legal profession is both an exciting and an anxious time for most young lawyers. There are challenges at every turn. And there are pressures. There are pressures from those for whom we work; from clients or adversary lawyers with whom we engage; and for those who may be starting families at the same time, there are personal pressures. Assignments in unfamiliar areas of law, the desire to do well, and criticisms from superiors all add to these pressures. The forgiving environment that the new lawyer grew accustomed to in college, and even to an extent in law school, is absent. Even with some senior-lawyer direction, you are largely on your own without much guidance. Most of your encounters in the academic world have been with rational people. For the first time, you may have to deal with seemingly irrational people, many of whom have motives or interests adverse to yours, both within your organization and outside of it. As lawyers progress in their careers, they have to venture even further into uncharted waters. They often face ethical dilemmas—for example, when an important client demands that a lawyer take a certain action while ethical rules suggest saying no. No senior lawyer in a profession can counsel new lawyers on every permutation of interactions the lawyer may have.

One aspect of professionalism that came into particular focus in the 1990s was lawyer civility. Instances of "Rambo" incivility between lawyers were being reported in the legal press. Bar associations in several states were taking notice, including our Commercial and Federal Litigation Section of the State Bar in New York, and considering steps to address this. Underlying this concern was the threat that rampant incivility posed to the public's confidence in the legal system if we could not police ourselves. There was also concern that the court system might intervene to impose restrictions on lawyers. In response, our Section composed a set of guidelines to instruct lawyers on certain principles that should guide the behavior of both lawyers and judges. We felt the practical approach to gaining acceptance was to make these guidelines precatory—basically instructional—and not to serve as a basis for sanctions or punishment.

When these proposed guidelines were first presented to the State Bar House of Delegates, they received a cool reception. The Section asked me to take a second try. I traveled to Albany the day before the meeting and casually walked into the two bars where I knew delegates would be engaged in hard thinking and tried to warm them up to our cause. The next day the measure passed by a narrow vote.

The next step was a meeting with the Office of Court Administration. At our urging, the Administrative Board adopted a code virtually identical to what we proposed. It remains as

Appendix A to Part 1200, our Rules of Professional Conduct. These Standards of Civility serve as a guide for lawyers who look for positive assurance that when they take the high road in their interaction with the bench and bar, they are acting in the best traditions of professionalism.

In 2016, I was asked to give the commencement speech at Touro Law School. That school has as its mission providing a legal education to many who either could not afford to attend other law schools or who had entered other lines of work and seek out a legal education as an aid in their work. Before preparing my remarks, I asked Dean Patricia Salkin to assemble a small group of graduating students for a brown-bag lunch at the school. One by one, they told me their individual stories. I was impressed that many of these students were aspiring to make their legal education an adjunct to their efforts to help their community. One woman was running a rape crisis center on Long Island. Another student was assisting veterans of Iraq and Afghanistan. And so on. In my remarks, I told the graduates what I felt would be the most important guideposts as they entered the world of law practice. Here is what I said:

> The Challenge of Professionalism. Now, professionalism is a word that may be familiar to you, but it's probably mostly a thought in the background, one of those nice-sounding attributes that one should stive for. But let me give you a different take on the meaning of "professional." For those of you who remember your history, over a period of centuries people in the so-called learned professions such as law, medicine, accountancy, architecture, and others achieved a high station

in our society. They each developed their own codes of ethics and standards of professional conduct. The coin of the realm for such professional people was not money, but the respect and admiration that the public held for people who were devoted to their education and their careers and allowed them to serve the public. Doctors made house calls on nights and weekends, and they didn't return home until all their patients had been seen. Lawyers helped clients in need and charged them only what they could pay. Professionals were different from others; they rose above the so-called morals of the marketplace and earned the trust of those they served.

I would like to recall for you an incident that stands out in my mind several years ago that illustrates the difference between lawyers and many others. I was attending a bar conference in New York City at a hotel where many sections of the New York State Bar were holding their annual meeting. There must have been a thousand lawyers there on a particular day, and as I got in the elevator with several of my colleagues, all of us wearing name tags that you are all familiar with, several businessmen were on the opposite side of the elevator and seeing our name tags one of the businessmen said to me, "Did you lawyers learn a lot about making money this morning in your meetings?" And I said, "No, I attended a session on legal ethics, my friend here attended a lecture on changes in the laws of wills and estates, and my other friend here gave a talk on his group effort to set up a *pro bono* clinic to assist people who could not afford to pay for legal services." And what had the businessmen attended? They had attended a session on building profitability through mergers and reductions of the work force—in other words, making money by firing employees after a corporate merger. So as the doors to that elevator opened, I walked out and said to myself, I am so glad I am a professional.

But in recent decades, there have been some alarming trends that you need to be aware of that impact professionalism in the world that you are entering. Professionalism is on attack from within as well as from without. Partners who may have spent their entire life in a law firm because legal skills are respected…are now being evaluated primarily by the amount of business they generate and the number of hours they bill. And if they don't meet these so-called metrics, they are pushed out. Associates are often not given the training that the firms once prided themselves in because neither the firm's clients nor the firm are willing to absorb the cost involved in helping a new lawyer write a brief or memo or attend court to learn from more experienced lawyers. And unlike in the past, when an arguable conflict of interest would preclude a law firm from representing a particular client, and the firm would then decline the representation, today a law firm is likely to fight tooth and nail to keep the matter and oppose a motion to disqualify the firm based on the claimed conflict.

Let me give you an example to illustrate my point about the decline of professionalism. You may remember a decade ago, a major energy company, Enron—remember Enron? Well, it failed spectacularly, and some people went to jail. Enron's accounting firm at the time was one of the world's largest, Arthur Andersen & Company, which had failed to detect Enron's fraudulent business practices, and the accounting firm was indicted for destroying documents and soon went out of business. And it was observed at the time that the professionalism that once was associated with that accounting firm had declined. Why? Well, when Mr. Arthur Andersen started the accounting firm many decades before, partners in the firm were compensated based on the quality of their work and their dedication to client service. Decades later, as in so many other professional organizations, the firm's compensation system had changed. Partners were now compensated based on the revenue they brought in from clients. While given these financial incentives and disincentives, the partners overseeing the Enron account were disincentivized to find any problems with Enron's financial accounting, because had they raised these problems with Enron's management, the accounting firm might be fired. And they, the partners overseeing the Enron account, would suffer financially if the Enron account were lost. So much for the independence of so-called independent accountants.

So, what will professionalism mean for you? Let me suggest the following:

- Professionalism is taking to heart and keeping on your desk the New York Code of Professional Conduct that governs our practice of law.
- Professionalism is always using your independent judgment while taking into account the views of others.
- Professionalism is saying no when your client tells you to do something that is not in accord with what you believe is right.
- Professionalism is doing your best at all times, but being willing to admit your mistakes, for it is by making mistakes that we learn.
- Professionalism is holding your temper when a lawyer adversary or even a judge in court says something that offends you.

But it is also speaking up if the circumstances dictate that you do so.

- Professionalism is acting civilly toward lawyers representing clients adverse to your clients even if you do not like or respect those lawyers. You will not only respect yourself for this, but you will find that over time, even your adversaries will refer clients to you because they respect you.
- Professionalism is keeping your promise when you make a commitment to a client or a colleague.
- And professionalism is remembering that if you speak at all, you will speak the truth.

Your reputation is your most valuable possession and has been said it takes a lifetime to acquire a reputation but only a moment to lose it. So please remember, respect yourself and those around you. If you do that, you will succeed no matter what path you may follow. Rest assured; the financial compensation will follow. If you respect your work and you respect yourself for the way you do it, you will not only succeed, but you will experience a lifetime of satisfaction in your chosen profession. Thank you for the opportunity to speak with you, and my best wishes to all of you.

My opportunity to meet with Touro students led me to create two scholarships at the law school. One of the great benefits of giving counsel to younger people is that you not only give them the benefit of your experience, but that you reaffirm for yourself the importance of the advice you give to others. I hope I have been as much the beneficiary of my advice as those who may have listened to me.

CHAPTER 45
FINAL WORDS

If you have read this far, then I have been privileged to share with you my journey of over seventy-five years, more than fifty of which have been spent in the trenches in the world of litigation and dispute resolution. There is a familiar saying: The more you learn, the more you realize you don't know. Although I have represented many clients, both public and private, and have participated in hundreds of trials, appeals, and other court appearances, I have learned something on every occasion to help me be a better lawyer. Like medical doctors who treat their patients with whatever illnesses they bring, lawyers do our best to bring resolution to people who come to us in conflict. That will always be my personal mission.

For those readers who are lawyers early in their career, I hope the account of my experiences will be of use to you as you advance in the profession. Despite the forces that have combined to challenge professionalism, I remain optimistic that the practice of law will continue to embody principles that inspire us and guide our conduct. Our society, and you, will be the beneficiary of that.

Chronicling one's life is an interesting experience. Looking back allows you to reflect on life's blessings and appreciate the simple fact that you have been granted the privilege of a long life. There have been great moments and, of course, not-so-great moments—even painful ones. But when friends and colleagues ask me if I plan to stop practicing law, I always respond, "No. I am just getting started."